INSTRUCTOR'S MANUAL AND TEST BANK

to accompany

Active Vocabulary
General and Academic Words
Fourth Edition

Amy E. Olsen
Cuesta College

Longman

New York   Boston   San Francisco
London   Toronto   Sydney   Tokyo   Singapore   Madrid
Mexico City   Munich   Paris   Cape Town   Hong Kong   Montreal

Instructor's Manual and Test Bank to accompany Olsen, *Active Vocabulary: General and Academic Words, Fourth Edition*

Copyright ©2010 Pearson Education, Inc.

All rights reserved. Printed in the United States of America. Instructors may reproduce portions of this book for classroom use only. All other reproductions are strictly prohibited without prior permission of the publisher, except in the case of brief quotations embodied in critical articles and reviews.

1 2 3 4 5 6 7 8 9 10–CW–12 11 10 09

Longman is an
imprint of

www.pearsonhighered.com

ISBN: 0-205-63279-3

Table of Contents

Preface

The *Instructor's Manual* features three components to enhance your use of *Active Vocabulary*: collaborative activities, games, and a test bank.

Collaborative Activities: This section suggests ways to use the Interactive Exercises in pairs, in small groups, or with the whole class. The section also introduces other activities that students can do together. These activities allow students to work with others, use the words in conversational settings, and discover their learning style preferences. Working with others can make students more comfortable with learning and using new words, which will lead to greater motivation to study vocabulary.

Games for Any Chapter: The use of games helps to show students that learning vocabulary should be enjoyable. The games range from group to individual. Some have winners, and some are "just for fun." The instructions explain what equipment is needed and how the games can be played. The games can be used for a single chapter or to review several chapters. Some of the games take advantage of the flash cards the students have made. Some games can take a whole class session to play, while others can be played in 15-20 minutes. If there isn't time to play any games in class, and there is student interest in using games as a review method, the instructor can make copies of a game's instructions to give to students so they can play with their friends, classmates, or as part of a study group session.

Test Bank: Three quizzes are provided for each chapter. The quizzes can be used for different semesters or for different sections of the course. There are also two quizzes for each Word Parts chapter and tests for the Review chapters and final exams. The tests are designed so that instructors can give them in various ways: the students can write the words in the blanks, put a letter in a blank space, or use a scan-tron form. Following the Test Bank is an Answer Section for all the exercises and tests in *Active Vocabulary* and in the *Instructor's Manual*.

Combining the materials in the text and the *Instructor's Manual* will help students see that learning vocabulary is not something to dread, but an activity to enjoy.

ALSO AVAILABLE

Active Vocabulary **Web Site**: The Web site features additional exercises and tests that allow for even more interaction between the student and the words. The Web site also has an audio component—students can listen to each chapter's thematic reading, and they can hear the pronunciation of each word as many times as they choose.

v

Collaborative Activities

Activities Using the Interactive Exercises

Collaborative learning gets students talking and leads to congenial classroom experiences that motivate students to attend class. Group projects can also help students to meet others they may want to form study groups with, which frequently result in life-long friendships. There are many ways to use the Interactive Exercises for collaborative activities. Suggested activities and chapters for which they may best be suited follow.

Pairs

Students work in pairs to create or share the Interactive Exercise. Students may work better together on some of the more creative topics, such as writing a science fiction story for Chapter 6. The students can also share their individual responses with another person orally or through further writing activities. Writing works especially well with the Interactive Exercises that ask for longer responses (Chapters 3, 6, 11, 19, 22, and 24). For example, in Chapter 3, a student can write a letter agreeing or disagreeing with the opinions presented in his or her partner's film or restaurant review. For Chapter 22, students can write replies to the friend's request to go to the spa/clinic for the weekend. The additional writing projects should also use the vocabulary words. Favorite correspondences can be shared with the whole class. Pairs can also continue to share their opinions related to an Interactive Exercise by using the vocabulary words in a conversation.

Small Groups

Small-group exercises give students a chance to use the words conversationally. Most of the Interactive Exercises work well in groups of four to six. Students can complete the Interactive Exercise in a small group, such as being a team organized to write the business plan for Chapter 20. Small groups can share their answers orally with each other and then pick favorite responses to share with the class. To enhance critical thinking skills, the members of each group can be asked to explain why they made their selections to share with the class. For example, for Chapter 12, students can explain what made the person's interview questions special or for Chapter 2, question 1, what made the response especially insightful.

Whole Class

Some of the Interactive Exercises can be done with the whole class participating. These exercises can be shared orally or on the board. A long list can be created on the board or a set number of answers (such as six) need to be given before moving on to the next question. The Interactive Exercises done individually can be shared by having students write one or two of their responses to a listing exercise (Chapters 8, 17, 25) on the board. When several responses are recorded, similar and different answers can be discussed. This activity also works well for the question format exercises (Chapters 1, 2, 7, 13, 14, 18, 20, and 23). A student can answer out loud or be assigned a question to write his or her response on the board. Discussion can follow as a variety of answers are presented.

Other Activities

The following activities can be used for individual chapters or for review of several chapters. They take advantage of different learning styles by employing art, writing, movement, and group work.

Design a Poster

Equipment needed: pens, colored markers or crayons, and unlined paper (large pieces preferred)

In small groups or individually, have the students design posters related to the reading topic. The students should use at least five words on the poster as well as draw people or images that will attract the public's attention and get their message across. Share the posters with the rest of the class. Have the class vote for the most persuasive poster. Possible chapter uses: 3 (advertise a movie or restaurant), 6-8 (advertise a science fiction, romance, or mystery novel), 20 (market the new business courses), 22 (announce a holistic-health fair), and 25 (publicize the Summer Theater Festival).

Snap Shots

Equipment needed: flash cards, paper, pens, and pictures (postcards, family photographs, ads, or pictures from magazines)

The instructor can provide the pictures or ask the students to bring them. The activity can involve groups of three to four people or be done individually. Give each group three or four pictures. The group members write a short (one paragraph) story for each picture. The students use four vocabulary words in each story. Share the pictures and stories with the class. If done individually, the instructor holds up three pictures, and the student picks one to write about. The student uses four words in his or her story. The pictures can be passed around if people need a closer look at them. When students have finished that paragraph, choose another three pictures and play another round. When the students have written three stories, share some of the stories with the class. Discuss how the same picture produces different stories and different uses of the vocabulary words.

Flash Card Story

Equipment needed: flash cards

Divide the class into groups of four to six people, and give each person one or two flash cards depending on how many words are being reviewed. The group then creates a story using the words. After roughly five minutes, each group presents its story to the class. Each person displays his or her word(s) when it appears in the story. One person can tell the entire story and the others can hold up their flash cards when appropriate, or each person can tell the part of the story that has his or her word(s) in it. Class members can vote for the stories they liked best or found the funniest or other categories with people explaining why they made their choices.

2

Hidden Story

Equipment needed: paper and pens, a board, and chalk or markers

Divide the class into groups (about five students per group). Write five words on one side of the board and five on the other side. The groups use the list on their side of the room. Give the class the topic. Each person writes a sentence using the first vocabulary word from the list on his or her side of the room. End the sentence with the last two words on a separate line so the paper can be folded with only the two words showing. These words are the only clue the next person has as to what has been written. The second person now writes a sentence using the second vocabulary word, and follows the same folding procedure. Go around the circle until all five words have been used. When the first person gets his or her original paper back, unfold it and read the story to the group. The resulting stories should be amusing. The stories also show how important it is for a writer to have an idea of what he or she wants to say to make a clear point. Share the story the group likes best with the rest of the class. Students can use other forms of the vocabulary words, such as plurals and past tense.

Possible topics and titles: The Adventures of a College Student, The Critic's Last Word, An Exciting Weekend, Staying Fit, A Person to Admire

Join Me

Equipment needed: flash cards

One person stands in front of the class holding a word and using it in a sentence. For example, if Anthony has the word diligent, he could say, "At this point in the semester, I feel I am a diligent student because I study regularly." He then asks, "Who can join me?" Anyone who can use a vocabulary word and add to Anthony's comment comes forward. Suzanne comes up and says, "I am also able to cope with work and school because I too study every night." And she asks anyone to join her. The activity continues until the whole class surrounds the first person. The group members can decide if they don't think a comment relates to the one before it, and therefore the person shouldn't be allowed to join the others yet. The students can pick their words from any of the vocabulary words to be studied for the session, or they can be limited to picking two or three flash cards to use before the activity begins.

Games for Any Chapter

These games can be used for individual chapters, the review chapters, or for midterm and final review sessions.

Charades

Equipment needed: flash cards

Pick a word from the flash card pile and show it to a student to act out for the class. Because some students are shy, it helps to divide the class into two teams and have one person from each team come up at the same time and act out the same word. The class can watch both actors to guess the word.

Picture This

Equipment needed: a board, chalk or markers, and flash cards

Divide the class into two teams. One student from each team comes to the board and is shown a flash card of the same word. They both draw something to represent the word. The two teams try to guess the word, using either drawing for clues.

Hangperson

Equipment needed: a board, chalk or markers, and flash cards

Divide the class into thirds. Draw a gallows on the board. One person comes to the front and picks a card from the flash-card pile. The student draws spaces on the board representing the letters of the word. One person from team one guesses a letter. If the letter is in the word, the student writes it in the appropriate space. Another person from the same team is given a chance to guess a letter. If the letter is not in the word, the student writes the letter on the board and draws a head on the gallows. Team two now guesses a letter. Members of the team keep guessing until someone misses a letter. Whenever a team misses a letter, draw another body part on the figure. If a team thinks it knows the word and it is the team's turn to guess a letter, the team can guess the word instead. If the team is wrong, it loses its turn. If the team is right, it gets a point. The team gets an extra point if it can give the definition of the word. The team the drawer came from gets a point if none of the teams guesses the word before a head, a body, two arms, two legs, two eyes, a nose, and a mouth are drawn.

4

Give an Example

Equipment needed: slips of paper, a bowl or other container, paper and pens

Assign each student a word. The student writes an example of the word on a slip of paper. For instance, if the word is <u>antonym,</u> a student could write "beautiful/ugly." The student puts his or her name and the assigned word on the other side of the slip. Put all of the slips into a bowl or other container. Each student numbers a sheet of paper 1 to 15. Pull out one of the examples and read it to the class. The students put the word they think the example shows next to number 1 on their sheets. Continue on through number 15. Then return to the slips and tell what word each slip illustrates. If there is some confusion, ask the person who wrote the slip to explain his or her example. The person with the most correct answers wins. If there are slips left, use more than 15 numbers on the sheets or play two rounds.

Six Guesses

Equipment needed: flash cards

Divide the class in half. Arrange two sets of desks facing each other at the front of the room. Invite two people from each team to sit in the desks. Show one person from each team a flash card. Pick a team to go first. The person who saw the word gives the other person a one-word clue to get him or her to guess the word. For example, if the word was <u>prioritize</u>, the person might say, "order." If the person guesses the word with one clue, the team gets six points. If the person doesn't guess the correct word, the next team gives a one-word clue. This time the clue might be "importance." If the team guesses the word, it gets five points. Continue the rotation of giving one-word clues and lowering the point value until a team gets the word or there aren't any points left. If no one gets the word, tell what the word was and call up another set of four and start with a new word.

Fit the Discipline

Equipment needed: flash cards, a Word List, or the Glossary

Give a student a flash card or a word and the name of a discipline or subject, and ask him or her to create a sentence or two that connects the word to the discipline. For example, if Elaine gets <u>access</u> and <u>chemistry</u>, she could say, "By studying <u>chemistry,</u> we have <u>access</u> to information that could do away with diseases."

Possible disciplines: administration of justice, art, astronomy, biology, business, chemistry, composition, computer science, drama, education, environmental science, French, geography, geology, history, literature, mathematics, nursing, physical education, political science, psychology, sociology, Spanish, speech, urban planning, zoology.

5

Opposites

Equipment needed: none (flash cards, a Word List, or the Glossary can be used for reference)

Divide the class in half and stand the students against facing walls. One team is the positive side and the other the negative side. Take turns starting with positive and negative comments. If the negative side starts, the first person in line makes a negative statement using one of the vocabulary words to be studied, for example: "I <u>loathe</u> doing homework." Someone on the positive side has to make a statement showing an opposite point of view while using a vocabulary word. The statements can be imaginative. For example, "I think doing homework is a <u>remarkable</u> way to spend my time." If the class agrees that the statements show opposite views, then both people sit down. If the statement doesn't work, someone else from the opposing side tries to make a statement. After three tries, if no one makes an opposite statement, the game proceeds to the next person in line who makes a new statement. Any students left standing after everyone has had a chance to make a statement are dubbed the least contrary people in the class.

Word Race

Equipment needed: Word Lists for the chapters to be studied or the Glossary, a board, and chalk or markers

This is a good game to revive a sluggish class or involve kinesthetic learners. Pull out three people and then divide the class in half. The group of three acts as judges; the other two groups can be given names based on two of the vocabulary words to be studied, such as the *amiable* and the *dependable* for Chapter 2. The *amiable* line up on one side of the room and the *dependable* on the other, facing the board (you may have to push back the desks for this game). Using the Word List or Glossary, give a definition of a word. The first person on each team runs to write the word on the board. The judges (standing at the side of the room) yell out "good studying" if the word is right or "study harder" if the answer is wrong, or they can use other lively phrases agreed upon by the class. Each team has one chance to write the word on the board. A team gets a point if the word is right. One of the judges writes the scores on the board.

Bingo

Equipment needed: Bingo sheets, flash cards, and markers (pennies work well)

Photocopy the Bingo sheet. The students bring in the flash cards for the chapters to be studied. After shuffling the flash cards, each student picks 25 random words and writes those on the card (24 words if there is a free middle space). They also need 24 or 25 markers. The instructor reads a definition. When students think a definition fits one of their words, they cover the word with the marker. A student shouts "Bingo!" when he or she has a line across, down, or diagonal. The instructor goes over the definitions and marked words to make sure the "Bingo" is valid.

B	I	N	G	O

7

Give Me a Clue

Equipment needed: paper and pens

Divide the class into small groups and give each group three words. The group writes three examples for each word. One group then goes to the front of the class and gives its first clue for a word. The spokesperson for each team raises a hand if the team thinks it knows the word. If the team gets it right on the first guess, that team and the clue-making team get 20 points and another team comes to the front. If no one gets it right, go to the second clue. On the second clue both teams get 15 points, and on the third clue they get 10 points. If no one gets it right after the third clue, tell what the word was and no one gets any points. Move on to another team's clues. If there is time, all the teams will present three words. The team with the highest score at the end wins.

If the word was blunder, a team's clues (examples) could be taking the lid off a blender while it is on, oversleeping on the day of an exam, and losing the phone number of someone you liked at a party.

At Random

Equipment needed: flash cards

Place students in small groups (about six people). One person picks a flash card from the pile and says a random word. The person then calls on a group member to make a connection between the vocabulary word and the random word. For example, Matt selects the word declare and says, "pumpkin." He then calls on Colleen, who replies, "I declare that pumpkin is my favorite kind of pie, especially with whipped cream on it." The person gets a point if the group agrees that the sentence makes sense using the two words. Pass the flash cards to the person on the right. Play until everyone has been called on three times. Reshuffle the cards after they have been gone through once. The person with the most points wins.

At Random in a Sack

Equipment needed: one large paper sack or several small ones (for small-group play), a variety of objects, and flash cards

Instead of using random words, ask the students to bring in various objects. The instructor may want to provide some additional objects. Put the objects in a sack (as many as will comfortably fit). Without looking inside, one student reaches into the sack and pulls out an object. The student also picks the top vocabulary word from the flash-card stack. The person then connects the object and the word. For example, if Gerry pulls out a bell and gets the word allot, he could say, "I am going to allot two hours to study for my history test, and I will ask my brother to ring a bell when my time is up." The person gets a point if the connection makes sense. Another person then takes a turn.

8

TEST BANK

Name _____   Class _____   Date _____

Chapter 1—Quiz 1

Pick the vocabulary word that best completes the sentence.

____ 1. Chocolate has become the _____ of my existence now that I am trying to lose
weight.
a. apathy   b. syllabus   c. bane   d. terminology

____ 2. I wanted to leave a voice mail for my professor, but I couldn't find my _____,
which has her phone number on it.
a. durable   b. syllabus   c. apathy   d. terminology

____ 3. I often _____ myself when I take a test by assuming I will do poorly instead
of reassuring myself that I have studied enough.
a. syllabus   b. comprise   c. indicate   d. undermine

____ 4. The concert will _____ music from a variety of countries, including
Austria, Tanzania, Argentina, and Cambodia.
a. berated   b. comprise   c. indicated   d. undermined

____ 5. When Tom came home with a huge dent in the car, his father _____ him.
a. indicated   b. berated   c. comprised   d. undermined

____ 6. The relationship appeared to be a _____ one: the couple really cared about
each other.
a. durable   b. zealous   c. bane   d. berated

____ 7. I feel better about a subject when I have learned its basic _____.
a. bane   b. syllabus   c. durable   d. terminology

____ 8. I was _____ about cleaning my house, and by the end of the weekend, it
was spotless.
a. zealous   b. durable   c. apathy   d. terminology

____ 9. All my aptitude tests _____ a talent for business, but I want to study
art.
a. comprise   b. undermine   c. berate   d. indicate

____ 10. Theresa's _____ toward her schoolwork led to her flunking all her classes.
a. syllabus   b. terminology   c. apathy   d. bane

Name _____   Class _____   Date _____

Chapter 1—Quiz 2

For each set, pick the vocabulary word that best completes the sentence. Use each word once.

SET 1

    a. undermine   b. syllabus   c. terminology   d. apathy   e. bane

___ 1. The teacher gave us a(n) _____ at the first class meeting that outlined
       assignments for the semester.

___ 2. When I was young, I considered my little brother the_____ of my
       existence, but now I appreciate his company.

___ 3. Our opponents tried to _____ our confidence by stealing our mascot the
       night before the big game.

___ 4. Due to voter _____, the measure didn't pass. People in town just didn't care
       about politics anymore.

___ 5. I had a difficult time learning the _____ in my geology class. I just
       couldn't get excited about learning the names for rocks.

SET 2

    a. zealous   b. indicate   c. comprise   d. durable   e. berating

___ 6. I need a suitcase that is _____. I plan to do a lot of traveling in the next few
       years.

___ 7. My history teacher said the midterm will _____ both multiple-choice
       and essay questions.

___ 8. The man was obviously a(n) _____ sports fan; every room in his house
       contained photographs or souvenirs related to sports.

___ 9. I hate to tell Maria when she has made a small error. She ends up _____ herself
       all day over the slightest mistake.

___ 10. The empty food containers and pile of dirty clothes _____ that my son
        stopped by the house this afternoon..

11

Name _____   Class _____   Date _____

Chapter 2—Quiz 1

Pick the vocabulary word that best completes the sentence.

___ 1. I have a(n) _____ for sweets that I need to control or my teeth will rot.
    a. serenity   b. affinity   c. mercenary   d. dour

___ 2. I thought my friends were more _____, but on the day we were to work on our project, they both made other plans.
    a. amiable   b. fruitful   c. dependable   d. mercenary

___ 3. Sometimes Marisa is too _____. She needs to tell her boyfriend that she hates horror movies and doesn't want to see them anymore.
    a. fruitful   b. dependable   c. dour   d. submissive

___ 4. The meeting was _____; we designed all the publicity fliers for the lecture series.
    a. dour   b. fruitful   c. amiable   d. submissive

___ 5. Octavio is so _____ that he won't even tell you the time of day without being paid.
    a. amiable   b. dour   c. submissive   d. mercenary

___ 6. I wanted to _____ the good student, so I studied hard and was always prepared for class.
    a. exemplify   b. serenity   c. affinity   d. discreet

___ 7. I tried to be _____ in asking my questions, but my friends figured out that I wanted information on the plans for my birthday party.
    a. dour   b. discreet   c. mercenary   d. submissive

___ 8. _____ has not been part of my life since I decided to take four classes and work full-time.
    a. Serenity   b. Fruitful   c. Affinity   d. Mercenary

___ 9. My teacher's _____ expression prevented my asking him any questions about the homework.
    a. dour   b. dependable   c. amiable   d. submissive

___ 10. The dinner party went well because I was able to get eight _____ people together.
    a. fruitful   b. mercenary   c. amiable   d. dour

Name _____   Class _____   Date _____

Chapter 2—Quiz 2

For each set, pick the vocabulary word that best completes the sentence. Use each word once.

SET 1

       a. discreet   b. serenity   c. exemplifies   d. affinity   e. fruitful

____ 1. I found _____ on a tropical island under a moonlit sky.

____ 2. The discussion was _____; we worked out a lot of our differences.

____ 3. I was so proud when my teacher told me that my paper _____ the kind of thinking he likes to see in students.

____ 4. The couple decided they should be _____ until they were ready to tell their friends about their feelings for each other.

____ 5. My friends think I'm strange, but I have a(n) _____ for math. I get excited solving equations.

SET 2

       a. dour   b. submissive   c. amiable   d. mercenary   e. dependable

____ 6. Charlie was a(n) _____ dog. He got up to greet everyone who visited the house.

____ 7. After obedience school, the dog was _____ to all of its master's commands.

____ 8. Because she is _____, I am not worried about my friend forgetting to pick me up at the airport.

____ 9. After a week of rain, it was understandable why the children wore _____ expressions.

____ 10. The _____ supported the war as long as he was paid.

Name _____ Class _____ Date _____

Chapter 3—Quiz 1

Pick the vocabulary word that best completes the sentence.

___ 1. Stewart has a(n) _____ to meeting new people, so he refused to come out of his room to meet his mother's guests.
    a. intrigue   b. aversion   c. ovation   d. protocol

___ 2. The employees were afraid that the new management would be _____ and would try to control their every move.
    a. virtual   b. clandestine   c. omnipresent   d. protocol

___ 3. The _____ ride made me feel as if I really were under water.
    a. virtual   b. intrigue   c. clandestine   d. omnipresent

___ 4. When the ambassador didn't follow _____ upon arriving in the country, the king was angered.
    a. ovation   b. aversion   c. intrigue   d. protocol

___ 5. My _____ host had candles ready when the lights went out.
    a. clandestine b. omnipresent   c. virtual   d. resourceful

Match the word to its definition.

___ 6. clandestine   a. wild or mad

___ 7. intrigue   b. to fascinate or a plot

___ 8. frenzied   c. a minor malfunction

___ 9. ovation   d. secret

___ 10. glitch   e. applause; approval

Name _____   Class _____   Date _____

Chapter 3—Quiz 2

For each set, pick the vocabulary word that best completes the sentence. Use each word once.

SET 1

        a. omnipresent   b. glitch   c. aversion   d. ovation   e. intrigued

____ 1. Samantha has a(n) _____ to crowds, so she doesn't enjoy going to sporting
       events.

____ 2. The possibility of a disaster at sea is _____ due to weather conditions and
       limited food supplies.

____ 3. What _____ me the most about taking the hike was the opportunity to see
       Silver Waterfall, which was supposed to be spectacular.

____ 4. For saving five children from a burning building, the city gave the fire-fighter a(n)
       _____.

____ 5. There was one _____ in my party-planning; I reversed the numbers in my
       address on the invitation and some people got lost.

SET 2

        a. frenzied   b. virtual   c. clandestine d. protocol   e. resourceful

____ 6. In my family, reunions are often _____ events with people wildly
       moving about and several loud conversations going on.

____ 7. I had to be _____ when I burned the cake just before the party began. I found
       a box of cookies in the cupboard and decorated them with icing and sprinkles, and the
       kids were just as happy.

____ 8. After a year, it was discovered that the secretary and treasurer of the club always
       conferred in a secret location an hour before the general meetings. We never
       understood why they needed these_____ meetings.

____ 9. Since half of the company moved to another state, we now hold _____
       meetings each week.

____ 10. When I took dance lessons, I learned the _____ for asking someone to
       dance at a fancy ball.

Name_____   Class_____   Date_____

Chapter 4—Quiz 1

Match the word part to its meaning. Use the sample words to help you make the connections.

Prefixes

____ 1. anti- (antipathy, antidote)

____ 2. circum- (circumvent, circumstances)

____ 3. trans- (transfer, translate)

Roots

____ 4. -cis- (concise, scissors)

____ 5. -claim- (exclaim, proclaim)

____ 6. -dur- (endure, durable)

____ 7. -fin- (final, definitive)

Suffixes

____ 8. -ary (mercenary, sedentary)

____ 9. -ify, -fy (modify, clarify)

____ 10. -ity (serenity, celebrity)

        a. hard   ab. to shout, to call out
        b. against   ac. around, on all sides
        c. end; limit   ad. quality, state of being
        d. to cut   ae. to make
        e. across   bc. pertaining to or connected with

Name_____   Class_____   Date_____

Chapter 4—Quiz 2

Match the word part to its meaning. Use the sample words to help you make the connections.

Prefixes

____ 1. circum- (circumvent, circumspect)

____ 2. anti- (antipathy, antidote)

____ 3. trans- (transmit, translate)

Roots

____ 4. -dur- (endure, durable)

____ 5. -claim- (exclaim, reclaim)

____ 6. -cis- (concise, incisive)

____ 7. -fin- (finalist, confine)

Suffixes

____ 8. -ity (serenity, duplicity)

____ 9. -ify, -fy (magnify, modify)

____ 10. -ary (mercenary, arbitrary)

a. hard   ab. to shout, to call out
b. against   ac. around, on all sides
c. end; limit   ad. quality, state of being
d. to cut   ae. to make
e. across   bc. pertaining to or connected with

Name_____   Class_____   Date_____

Chapter 5—Quiz 1

Pick the vocabulary word that best completes the sentence.

____1. My friend wanted to know if she should take a history class next semester, so I
showed her my _____ to give her an idea about the course requirements.
a. apathy   b. serenity   c. syllabus   d. glitch

____2. I left the important papers in Colleen's care because she is a _____ person.
a. durable   b. mercenary   c. frenzied   d. dependable

____ 3. The play equipment needs to be _____ because kids will be jumping on it
all day.
a. amiable   b. durable   c. dour   d. virtual

____ 4. After the team lost ten games in a row, there was a lot of _____ among the
fans. Hardly anyone showed up for the games anymore.
a. apathy   b. intrigue   c. serenity   d. ovation

____ 5. The _____ in the film class wasn't that hard to learn because we applied
most of the words to each film that we watched.
a. affinity   b. glitch   c. protocol   d. terminology

____ 6. The boss was so _____ that he wouldn't let an employee off to go to a
funeral.
a. resourceful b. zealous   c. discreet   d. mercenary

____ 7. Because I am the oldest child and I want my brothers and sisters to do well in school, I
try to _____ the behaviors of a good student
a. berate   b. intrigue   c. exemplify   d. undermine

____ 8. I need to stop being so_____ and speak up; otherwise, I will always have to eat
at the restaurants my boyfriend likes and never get to try the ones that interest me.
a. virtual   b. submissive   c. zealous   d. dour

____ 9. The author was _____ about promoting her new book. She traveled to fifty cities in
twenty days to give readings and sign her books.
a. clandestine b. zealous   c. fruitful   d. durable

____ 10. The children said they had a(n) _____ to vegetables, but after their mother dipped
the carrots and broccoli in Ranch dressing, the children loved them.
a. intrigue   b. affinity   c. bane   d. aversion

18

For each set, pick the vocabulary word that best completes the sentence.

      a. protocol   b. serenity   c. undermining   d. berate   e. omnipresent

____ 11. I try not to _____ myself when I make a mistake. Instead, I try to learn from it.
____ 12. Getting five hours of sleep a night was _____ Tim's health, but he refused to admit it.
____ 13. Coffee shops are _____ downtown: one can be found on every block.
____ 14. The _____ at my workplace requires showing an e-mail to one's supervisor before
      sending it to the entire office.
____ 15. My _____ was interrupted when the children came home ready to play.

      a. clandestine   b. frenzied   c. fruitful   d. resourceful   e. dour

____ 16. Searching through five years of newspapers turned out to be _____. The
      detective found the clue she needed.
____ 17. It was a _____ morning, but we got the house cleaned and decorated for the party.
____ 18. I decided not to ask the man for directions; his _____ look scared me.
____ 19. Marissa can be quite _____. She managed to get us tickets to the sold-out concert.
____ 20. Because of the low lighting, Sly's is the perfect café for _____ meetings.

Match the word to its definition.

____ 21. bane   a. simulated or almost existing
____ 22. ovation   b. fondness; liking
____ 23. comprise   c. something that ruins
____ 24. affinity   d. applause; approval
____ 25.virtual   e. to consist of

Finish the story using the vocabulary words. Use each word once.
      a. intrigue   b. discreet   c. indicated   d. amiable   e. glitch

There was only one (26.)_____ in my flight. When the plane was late taking off, I had
a feeling that there was some kind of (27.)_____ going on. After forty minutes, I was
sure that the delay (28.)_____ that something was seriously wrong with the plane or
the crew. I thought I should be (29.)_____ in asking what was wrong because I didn't
want to panic the other passengers. The man at the gate was very (30.)_____ and
quieted my fears when he told me that the plane was late due to bad weather in San Francisco.
      ____ 26.   ____ 27.   ____ 28.   ____ 29.   ____ 30.

Use the words below to help you match the word part to its meaning.

____ 31. circum-: circumvent, circumspect, circumstances   a. hard
____ 32. -ary: mercenary, sedentary, ordinary   b. to cut
____ 33. -dur-: durable, endure, obdurate   c. around, on all side
____ 34. -cis-: precise, concise, scissors   d. across
____ 35. trans-: transfer, translate, transmit   e. pertaining to

19

Name _____   Class _____   Date _____

Chapter 5—Quiz 2

Pick the vocabulary word that best completes the sentence.

___ 1. After the delivery van left, my _____ neighbor came over and offered to
help me put the bookcases together.
    a. dour   b. submissive   c. virtual   d. zealous

___ 2. I saw an ad for a(n)_____ game that allows a person to feel what it is like
to be an astronaut in outer space. I wonder where I can buy it.
    a. frenzied   b. omnipresent   c. virtual   d. dour

___ 3. Victor is usually quite _____, but when he is hungry, he can get grumpy.
    a. durable   b. resourceful   c. discreet   d. amiable

___ 4. Some fast-food chains have become _____. You can find them all over
the world.
    a. dour   b. omnipresent   c. durable   d. submissive

___ 5. Marcia is usually so _____ that I was surprised when she shouted to me across the
office, "How was your date with Harry?"
    a. discreet   b. frenzied   c. zealous   d. dour

___ 6. After surviving a serious illness, I decided to stop being so _____ and start
being more generous.
    a. durable   b. mercenary   c. dependable   d. clandestine

___ 7. The _____ in my computer class is all new to me. I have a lot of words and
abbreviations to learn this semester.
    a. protocol   b. apathy   c. mercenary   d. terminology

___ 8. The _____ look on her face told me that she had not done well on the test.
    a. dour   b. amiable   c. fruitful   d. mercenary

___ 9. A _____ caused the fireworks to start late, so the music and fireworks did not
coordinate as was planned, but most people still enjoyed the show.
    a. syllabus   b. serenity   c. glitch   d. protocol

___ 10. I have a(n) _____ to seafood, so fishing has never appealed to me as a hobby.
    a. intrigue   b. serenity   c. bane   d. aversion

For each set, pick the vocabulary word that best completes the sentence.

a. protocol   b. syllabus   c. affinity   d. bane   e. serenity

____ 11. To maintain my _____ while I had guests visiting, I took an hour walk each day.
____ 12. The _____ indicates all the test dates, so I have no excuse for being unprepared.
____ 13. I have a(n) _____ for flowers; I always have a bouquet next to my bed.
____ 14. I learned how to bow, so I could follow the accepted _____ for meeting the queen.
____ 15. The current _____ of my existence is the snow. It has made driving extremely hard these last three weeks.

a. indicates   b. comprises   c. exemplify   d. intrigues   e. berate

____ 16. The all-star team _____ athletes from six schools in the region.
____ 17. I plan to see the movie because what I have heard about the plot _____ me.
____ 18. I am no longer going to _____ myself when I make a simple mistake.
____ 19. I am proud to _____ the type of son that a parent can be proud of.
____ 20. I just learned that the flashing light on my phone _____ that I have a message.

Match the word to its definition.

____ 21. fruitful   a. secret; private
____ 22. resourceful   b. lasting; firm
____ 23. durable   c. successful; abundant
____ 24. clandestine   d. obedient; passive
____ 25. submissive   e. capable; inventive

Finish the story using the vocabulary words. Use each word once.
a. ovation   b. apathy   c. frenzied   d. dependable   e. undermining

I was surprised at how quickly my (26.)_____ toward music changed into a love of singing. I had been (27.)_____ my ability until my tenth-grade teacher encouraged me to try out for the choir. After the first semester, she said not only was my voice excellent, but I was also valuable to the choir because I was so (28.)_____. I never miss a rehearsal, and I always know all the words. The night before our big show was (29.)_____ as we finished up our costumes and smoothed out our dance steps. I was overjoyed when the audience gave us a standing (30.)_____. We really had put on an excellent performance.
____ 26.   ____ 27.   ____ 28.   ____ 29.   ____ 30.

Use the words below to help you match the word part to its meaning.

____ 31. -ify, -fy: modify, magnify, verify   a. to shout, to call out
____ 32. anti-: antipathy, antidote, antiseptic   b. against
____ 33. -claim-: proclaim, exclaim, reclaim   c. end, limit
____ 34. -ity: serenity, maternity, celebrity   d. quality, state of being
____ 35. -fin-: confine, definitive, final   e. to make

21

Name _____   Class _____   Date _____

Chapter 6—Quiz 1

Pick the vocabulary word that best completes the sentence.

___ 1. Our instruments are broken, so we can't make a _____ judgment as to our location.
    a. cursory   b. precise   c. omnipotent   d. annihilate

___ 2. One _____ and we could be lost forever.
    a. antipathy   b. emissary   c. dissent   d. miscalculation

___ 3. The captain was quite angry about the breakdown. He is not one to _____ mistakes.
    a. subjugate   b. condone   c. annihilate   d. dissent

___ 4. When a strange ship approached, we thought it was going to _____ us, but it turned out to be friendly and helped us repair our equipment.
    a. condone   b. annihilate   c. dissent   d. precise

___ 5. The _____ returned from his mission with sad news: the king was ill, and his recovery was unlikely.
    a. emissary   b. antipathy   c. dissent   d. miscalculation

___ 6. A _____ inspection of the plant found six major problems. The team members felt they would find even more when they returned for a closer inspection.
    a. precise   b. omnipotent   c. cursory   d. dissent

___ 7. Although she felt _____ toward her boss, she greeted him pleasantly every morning.
    a. emissary   b. antipathy   c. miscalculation   d. dissent

___ 8. The conquerors were able to _____ the nation for a while, but the people regained their freedom after a fierce battle.
    a. subjugate   b. dissent   c. condone   d. miscalculation

___ 9. I was the only one to _____. Everyone else thought the plan sounded great.
    a. dissent   b. annihilate   c. subjugate   d. condone

___ 10. The king thought he was _____, but when he taxed his people too much, they rebelled.
    a. cursory   b. precise   c. subjugate   d. omnipotent

Name _____   Class _____   Date _____

Chapter 6—Quiz 2

For each set, pick the vocabulary word that best completes the sentence. Use each word once.

SET 1

     a. dissent   b. subjugate   c. annihilated d. antipathy   e. emissaries

___ 1. It was robot against robot. Whichever one _____ the other would decide the fate of a nation.

___ 2. The _____ between the two countries had grown so strong that they decided the robot battle was the only way to settle their differences.

___ 3. The winning side would be allowed to _____ the losers.

___ 4. Without one word of _____, both sides had agreed to this plan.

___ 5. The contest began with opening remarks made by _____ from each country.

SET 2

     a. cursory   b. precise   c. omnipotent d. miscalculation   e. condone

___ 6. Each side had been _____ in programming its robot's fighting talents. Each wanted to make sure its robot was the best.

___ 7. Just before the fighting began, Franmany realized they had made a slight _____.

___ 8. They didn't have much time, so the programmers made a(n) _____ examination of their plan to see if they could change anything.

___ 9. The Engway said they would not _____ any delays; it was time to start the battle.

___ 10. In seconds, the Engway's robot smashed the Franmany robot, and the Engway became the _____ rulers of the Franmany people.

Name _____   Class _____   Date _____

Chapter 7—Quiz 1

Pick the vocabulary word that best completes the sentence.

___ 1. After a hard semester, all I wanted was to spend a week in _____, so I could rest.
    a. euphoria   b. seclusion   c. pandemonium   d. oblivious

___ 2. When Wanda won the lottery, _____ broke out in the house. Everyone was cheering, laughing, and crying for joy.
    a. seclusion   b. amorous   c. virile   d. pandemonium

___ 3. Max _____ senseless rules and fights to change them.
    a. abhors   b. deludes   c. provocative   d. embellishes

___ 4. Building the pyramids required the heavy labor of thousands of _____ men.
    a. oblivious   b. provocative   c. virile   d. amorous

___ 5. For our research paper, our teacher wanted us to pick a(n) _____ topic: something about which we could argue.
    a. oblivious   b. virile   c. amorous   d. provocative

___ 6. To make himself more employable, Albert _____ his resume by making his duties sound more important than they actually were.
    a. deluded   b. embellished   c. abhorred   d. secluded

___ 7. After a candlelight dinner, the couple felt _____.
    a. amorous   b. oblivious   c. abhor   d. virile

___ 8. I tried to _____ myself into believing that the math test had been unfair, but I really knew that my score was low because I hadn't studied enough.
    a. abhor   b. embellish   c. delude   d. provocative

___ 9. Ivana was _____ to the signs of her husband's cheating. She faced the truth only when she saw him kissing another woman.
    a. amorous   b. provocative   c. delude   d. oblivious

___ 10. After its team won the championship, the crowd waved banners and sang victory songs to display its _____.
    a. euphoria   b. pandemonium   c. seclusion   d. virile

Name _____   Class _____   Date _____

Chapter 7—Quiz 2

For each set, pick the vocabulary word that best completes the sentence. Use each word once.

SET 1

       a. virile   b. oblivious   c. abhorred   d. embellish   e. amorous

____ 1. Uncle Oscar always liked to _____ his stories, so I never knew how much to believe.

____ 2. One day he told me about his _____ neighbor, Hans, who could build a house by himself in two days.

____ 3. Hans had _____ feelings for Greta, but he didn't know how to tell her.

____ 4. In fact, Greta was _____ to Hans's feelings because Hans was too shy to show her that he liked her.

____ 5. Uncle Oscar usually _____ getting involved in romantic adventures, but he agreed to help Hans.

SET 2

       a. pandemonium   b. euphoria   c. provocative d. seclusion   e. delude

____ 6. Uncle Oscar decided _____ was important for Hans to tell Greta how he felt. At the town picnic, he arranged a private meeting between them in the woods.

____ 7. Unfortunately, Greta's parents reported her lost and _____ broke out at the picnic as everyone set out to find her.

____ 8. Greta's _____ upon hearing Hans's feelings was short-lived as a group of townspeople came rushing through the woods.

____ 9. Hans tried to _____ the crowd into believing he had just found Greta, but everyone could see what was going on.

____ 10. When one of the townspeople asked the _____ question regarding a wedding announcement, Hans and Greta blushed.

Chapter 8—Quiz 1

Pick the vocabulary word that best completes the sentence.

____ 1. Frank's _____ that something bad would happen to the ship turned out to be right. It sank an hour after leaving port.
    a. alibi   b. optimist   c. decisive   d. presentiment

____ 2. Samantha tried to _____ the steps to registering, but she was sent back to counseling to do the necessary paperwork.
    a. covert   b. assent   c. incredulous   d. circumvent

____ 3. Violet is such a(n) _____. Even when the power went out, she found a bright side: she lit a fire to make s'mores.
    a. optimist   b. incredulous   c. covert   d. decisive

____ 4. When my sister showed our parents the straight A's on her report card, they were _____. She had never been an excellent student before.
    a. covert   b. decisive   c. incredulous   d. transitory

____ 5. For Charles, love is often a(n) _____ feeling, but he is happy during the short time it lasts.
    a. covert   b. transitory   c. incredulous   d. circumvent

Finish the story using the vocabulary words. Use each word once.

    a. decisive   b. assent   c. alibi   d. misgivings   e. covert

Sam's (6.)_____ didn't hold up. His friend said he hadn't been with him on Monday night. I had had (7.)_____ about Sam's story all along. I was glad my chief had given his (8.)_____ to my watching Sam's house for another week. I conducted my (9.)_____ observation of his house from a hiding place across the street. I discovered that he had several visitors every night between nine and eleven. The visitors came with large sacks and left empty handed. I suspected that Sam had moved from stealing to buying stolen goods. When a large van arrived on Friday, I knew it was time for (10.)_____ action. I was sure Sam was planning to escape. I called my chief, and he agreed that it was time to make our move.

    ____ 6.   ____ 7.   ____ 8.   ____ 9.   ____ 10.

Name _____   Class _____   Date _____

Chapter 8—Quiz 2

For each set, pick the vocabulary word that best completes the sentence. Use each word once.

SET 1

      a. assent   b. optimist   c. alibi   d. misgivings e. presentiment

____ 1. I hope my friends don't investigate my _____ for being late to dinner. I said I had to do some extra work, but I really went to a sale.

____ 2. I wish I was more of a(n) _____, but I can only see disaster ahead for this weekend's ski trip.

____ 3. In the 1700s, several sailors had _____ about going on long voyages, but the spirit of adventure carried them away.

____ 4. When the wedding dress arrived with a hole in it and the flowers wilted two hours before the ceremony, I had a(n) _____ that this marriage was doomed.

____ 5. The invitation said that my host would be "thrilled" if I would _____ to spending the weekend at his cabin. With such a welcoming offer, I, of course, agreed to go.

SET 2

      a. covert   b. decisive   c. incredulous d. circumvent e. transitory

____ 6. It was wrong for the contractor to _____ the building codes. Because of his decision, thirty houses collapsed during the earthquake.

____ 7. Many people were _____ about the possibility of traveling to the moon, but it finally happened.

____ 8. When a conglomerate threatened to take over, the chairman of the board took _____ steps to save his company.

____ 9. Laura got suspicious when she discovered the _____ conversations her friends were having. She wondered what they were secretly planning.

____ 10. The pain is _____, but when it comes it hurts.

27

Name_____   Class_____   Date_____

Chapter 9—Quiz 1

Match the word part to its meaning. Use the sample words to help you make the connections.

Prefixes

____ 1. mis- (misgivings, mislead)

____ 2. omni- (omniscient, omnipresent)

____ 3. sub-, sup- (submerge, suppress)

Roots

____ 4. -cred- (credibility, credit)

____ 5. -pend-, -pens- (pendant, suspense)

____ 6. -sens-, -sent- (consensus, dissent)

____ 7. -vers-, -vert- (aversion, introvert)

Suffixes

____ 8. -ism (patriotism, pessimism)

____ 9. -ist (naturalist, arsonist)

____ 10. -ology (zoology, biology)

a. all   ab. a person who
b. the study of   ac. to believe, to trust
c. wrong   ad. to feel, to be aware
d. below, under   ae. action, practice, theory
e. to hang, to weigh, to pay   bc. to turn

Name_____ Class_____ Date_____

Chapter 9—Quiz 2

Match the word part to its meaning. Use the sample words to help you make the connections.

Prefixes

____ 1. sub-, sup- (submissive, suppress)

____ 2. omni- (omnipotent, omnipresent)

____ 3. mis- (miscalculation, mistake)

Roots

____ 4. -vers-, -vert- (controversy, covert)

____ 5. -sens-, -sent- (sensitive, dissent)

____ 6. -pend-, -pens- (suspend, expensive)

____ 7. -cred- (incredible, credibility)

Suffixes

____ 8. -ology (psychology, biology)

____ 9. -ism (patriotism, humanism)

____ 10. -ist (naturalist, artist)

a. all   ab. a person who
b. the study of   ac. to believe, to trust
c. wrong   ad. to hang, to weigh, to pay
d. below, under   ae. action, practice, theory
e. to turn   bc. to feel, to be aware

Name _____   Class _____   Date _____

Chapter 10—Quiz 1

Pick the vocabulary word that best completes the sentence.

____1. I had a great _____ for the time of the robbery: I was standing in front of one hundred people as the best man at a wedding.
    a. emissary   b. misgiving   c. alibi   d. euphoria

____2. The Blizzards _____ our team; the final score was 98-4.
    a. assented   b. deluded   c. circumvented   d. annihilated

____ 3. The _____ couple kept exchanging longing looks throughout the party, and just before midnight they were found holding hands on the balcony.
    a. cursory   b. amorous   c. transitory   d. precise

____ 4. I was _____ when my husband said he had already bought my birthday present. For the last ten years, he has run out on my birthday to find something to get me.
    a. virile   b. cursory   c. oblivious   d. incredulous

____ 5. The director was _____ on the set. Whatever he wanted he got.
    a. omnipotent b. provocative   c. precise   d. decisive

____ 6. I enjoy dining with Carlos because he always has a few _____ topics to discuss, which keeps the conversation lively.
    a. cursory   b. virile   c. covert   d. provocative

____ 7. I made one _____ in my monthly budget and ended up having to borrow $60 from a friend to get me through the month.
    a. misgiving   b. alibi   c. pandemonium   d. miscalculation

____ 8. My favorite part of being a spy is the _____ operations. I love wearing disguises.
    a. oblivious   b. omnipotent   c. covert   d. amorous

____ 9. The author went into _____ after his book was harshly criticized. He didn't want to see anyone for awhile.
    a. alibi   b. seclusion   c. presentiment   d. miscalculation

____ 10. The Romans were able to _____ several countries due to their disciplined armies.
    a. embellish   b. subjugate   c. assent   d. abhor

For each set, pick the vocabulary word that best completes the sentence.

a. optimist   b. emissary   c. euphoria   d. pandemonium e. antipathy

____ 11. My _____ was complete when my youngest child made it home for Thanksgiving. All three children were home for the first time in four years.
____ 12. His _____ toward advertising makes it hard to watch television.
____ 13. There was _____ in the store when shoes went on sale for half price.
____ 14. Ever the eternal _____; Pat thought she could write a quality paper in two days.
____ 15. The _____ returned from the mission with a peaceful solution to the matter.

a. dissent b. delude   c. condone   d. abhor   e. circumvent

____ 16. I was shocked that my friend would _____ me about his interest in my girlfriend.
____ 17. I had to _____. I couldn't agree that pink was a good color for the house.
____ 18. I _____ violence, so I won't watch boxing.
____ 19. Marissa found a way to _____ the usual methods and get us tickets to the sold-out concert with backstage passes.
____ 20. I don't _____ graffiti, even if it does sometimes look like art.

Match the word to its definition.

____ 21. presentiment   a. to agree
____ 22. embellish   b. foreboding
____ 23. assent   c. exact; accurate
____ 24. virile   d. manly; strong
____ 25. precise   e. to add details

Finish the story using the vocabulary words. Use each word once.

a. misgivings   b. oblivious   c. cursory   d. transitory   e. decisive

I had no idea that this was a(n) (26.)_____ game. If I had known, I wouldn't have given the equipment and clothes such a(n) (27.)_____ check. I had (28.)_____ about the team winning anyways, so I quickly looked over the helmets and other gear. When the quarterback found a crack in his helmet and another player a rip in his jersey, I tried to act (29.)_____ to the problems. Finally, the coach realized I had not been doing my job well, and, like so many other jobs, this one proved to be (30.)_____.

____ 26.   ____ 27.   ____ 28.   ____ 29.   ____ 30.

Use the words below to help you match the word part to its meaning.

____ 31. -sens-, -sent-: sensitive, sentimental, assent   a. below, under
____ 32. -ist: naturalist, journalist, optimist   b. the study of
____ 33. sub-, sup-: submerge, submissive, suppress   c. a person who
____ 34. -cred-: credentials, incredible, credit   d. to believe, to trust
____ 35. -ology: biology, psychology, zoology   e. to feel, to be aware

31

Name _____   Class _____   Date _____

Chapter 10—Quiz 2

Pick the vocabulary word that best completes the sentence.

___ 1. I had to _____ with the lunch plans: the last time I ate at the Tasty Tavern I got
      sick.
      a. assent   b. dissent   c. condone   d. annihilate

___ 2. Trying to _____ the rules or procedures often leads to more problems.
      a. embellish   b. subjugate   c. abhor   d. circumvent

___ 3. After an hour of discussing where to eat, Victor said he was hungry and that it was
      time for _____ action. He took us to his favorite restaurant.
      a. cursory   b. provocative   c. decisive   d. amorous

___ 4. Wrestling is usually considered to be a _____ sport.
      a. covert   b. virile   c. transitory   d. omnipotent

___ 5. I am always able to _____ myself into believing that I will eat only one
      chocolate chip cookie.
      a. delude   b. condone   c. embellish   d. circumvent

___ 6. I was quick to _____ when my sister asked if I wanted to go to the baseball
      game with her. I love going to the ballpark.
      a. abhor   b. assent   c. dissent   d. annihilate

___ 7. My third-grade teacher would not _____ messy writing. If she couldn't
      read a student's paper, she gave it back to be rewritten.
      a. delude   b. condone   c. subjugate   d. circumvent

___ 8. The operation was supposed to be _____, but the enemy was prepared;
      someone had given us away.
      a. covert   b. amorous   c. oblivious   d. precise

___ 9. Karla tends to _____ her stories. I knew that she had been to Washington,
      D.C., even if it wasn't true that she went to help the President with a crisis.
      a. abhor   b. embellish   c. delude   d. assent

___ 10. I have a(n) _____ toward eggs, so I am never that excited about going out to
      breakfast.
      a. emissary   b. euphoria   c. seclusion   d. antipathy

For each set, pick the vocabulary word that best completes the sentence.

a. emissary   b. miscalculation c. pandemonium   d. misgivings   e. presentiment

___ 11. I had _____ about the weekend, but we really had a good time together.
___ 12. The _____ traveled on three hundred missions during his six years on the job.
___ 13. I am tired of the _____ at work. I wish one day would go smoothly.
___ 14. Due to Ted's _____, by nightfall we were still eighty miles from our hotel.
___ 15. I had a strong _____ that my package was going to get lost in the mail.

a. oblivious   b. cursory   c. amorous d. transitory   e. omnipotent

___ 16. This heat wave is supposed to be _____; it should be over by the weekend.
___ 17. The _____ couple couldn't keep their hands off each other.
___ 18. My _____ survey of the motel room caused me to miss my slippers when we left.
___ 19. At times I wish I were _____ so I could control everyone in my life.
___ 20. I was _____ to the possible wind storm and surprised when the power went out.

Match the word to its definition.

___ 21. precise   a. stimulating; exciting
___ 22. incredulous   b. exact or demanding
___ 23. provocative   c. to conquer
___ 24. subjugate   d. a sheltered place
___ 25. seclusion   e. skeptical; doubtful

Finish the story using the vocabulary words. Use each word once.
a. annihilate   b. abhor   c. euphoria   d. alibi   e. optimist

I (26.)_____ secrets, and there was something mysterious going on in my family. My parents were whispering when I came to breakfast Tuesday morning. On Thursday, my brother came home two hours late. His friend provided a(n) (27.)_____ saying they were studying at the library, but that didn't seem realistic. I desperately wanted to find out what was going on. Usually I'm a(n) (28.)_____, but this time I wasn't sure that something good was about to happen. By Friday afternoon, I was ready to (29.)_____ anyone who prevented me from uncovering my family's plot. When I got home, I opened the door to a surprise party. My (30.)_____ was complete when I opened my last present: a new computer!
    ___ 26.   ___ 27.   ___ 28.   ___ 29.   ___ 30.

Use the words below to help you match the word part to its meaning.

___ 31. -ism: patriotism, voyeurism, plagiarism   a. all
___ 32. -vers-, -vert-: aversion, covert, avert   b. to turn
___ 33. omni-: omnipresent, omniscient, omnipotent   c. wrong
___ 34. mis-: misgiving, miscalculation, mistake   d. action, practice, theory
___ 35. -pend-, -pens-: suspend, spend, pensive   e. to hang, to weigh, to pay

33

Name _____ Class _____ Date _____

Chapter 11—Quiz 1

Pick the vocabulary word that best completes the sentence.

___ 1. I have been so _____ to illnesses this year that I am going to check with my
    doctor and see if something is wrong with my body.
    a. surpass   b. innate   c. susceptible   d. potential

___ 2. I have also been stressed at work, so that may have _____ my getting
    completely better.
    a. adhered   b. advocated   c. imposed   d. impeded

___ 3. The doctor told me that taking a week off from work would _____ my
    getting better.
    a. impede   b. facilitate   c. adhere   d. advocate

___ 4. It was hard for me at first to _____ to the doctor's schedule of rest and
    moderate exercise, but I managed to follow her plan, and I felt better at the end
    of the week.
    a. adhere   b. nurture   c. impose   d. impede

___ 5. Laurene thought her garden had the _____ to win first prize in the
    neighborhood contest.
    a. innate   b. adhere   c. potential   d. susceptible

___ 6. She had _____ gardening skills. Ever since she was a child, she could make
    things grow.
    a. innate   b. imposed   c. susceptible   d. potential

___ 7. The contest _____ rules on the types of flowers that could be grown.
    a. adhered   b. imposed   c. facilitated   d. nurtured

___ 8. Laurene spent a lot of time _____ her flowers, and they looked gorgeous.
    She won first prize.
    a. impeding   b. advocating   c. facilitating   d. nurturing

___ 9. My mother _____ herself with her latest birthday cake: a volcano that spewed
    ice cream.
    a. advocated   b. nurtured   c. impeded   d. surpassed

___ 10. Most health experts _____ exercising at least three times a week.
    a. adhere   b. advocate   c. impede   d. facilitate

Name _____   Class _____   Date _____

Chapter 11—Quiz 2

For each set, pick the vocabulary word that best completes the sentence. Use each word once.

SET 1

      a. impede   b. potential   c. surpass   d. nurture   e. facilitate

____ 1. To _____ a child's love of reading it helps to start early in life.

____ 2. Every child has the _____ to be a good reader.

____ 3. Parents shouldn't _____ a child's interest in reading by forcing certain books on the child.

____ 4. Parents can _____ the process of finding good books by taking their children to the library weekly and letting them choose from a variety of books.

____ 5. A child's interest in reading may even _____ a parent's expectations if the child finds books that really capture his or her interest.

SET 2

      a. innate   b. impose   c. adhere   d. advocate   e. susceptible

____ 6. Most experts _____ finding a form of exercise that your child likes to do.

____ 7. Parents shouldn't _____ the sport they love on their children.

____ 8. Some children are _____ athletes, while others take time to develop their skills.

____ 9. Children can be _____ to injuries, so the proper equipment should be worn at all times.

____ 10. If parents _____ to a few sensible rules, they can have kids who will love to exercise throughout life.

Name _____   Class _____   Date _____

Chapter 12—Quiz 1

Pick the vocabulary word that best completes the sentence.

____ 1. The platypus is _____ to Australia; it is one of the many unusual animals found on the continent.
   a. endemic   b. omnivorous   c. habitat   d. mammal

____ 2. The Earth will no longer be a friendly _____ if humans do not deal with the environmental dangers on the land and in the sea and air.
   a. mammal   b. habitat   c. moratorium   d. conservationist

____ 3. After the candidates began to give long speeches at lunch every day, the principal put a _____ on lunchtime campaigning.
   a. zoology   b. habitat   c. encroachment   d. moratorium

____ 4. On our hike through the woods, the _____ shared fascinating information on what is being done to protect the animals in the area.
   a. habitat   b. mammal   c. conservationist   d. elicit

____ 5. The giraffe is my favorite _____.
   a. endemic   b. omnivorous   c. habitat   d. mammal

Match the word to its definition.

____ 6. elicit   a. eating all types of food

____ 7. zoology   b. an intrusion

____ 8. avert   c. to prevent or to turn away

____ 9. omnivorous   d. the study of animals

____ 10. encroachment   e. to draw or bring out

Name _____   Class _____   Date _____

Chapter 12—Quiz 2

For each set, pick the vocabulary word that best completes the sentence. Use each word once.

SET 1

          a. elicit   b. avert   c. conservationist   d. omnivorous   e. endemic

____ 1. Lucy decided to become a(n) _____ because she wanted to save endangered plants and animals.

____ 2. I tried to _____ an answer from my husband on whether he wanted pizza or burritos for dinner, but I couldn't get a response while the football game was on.

____ 3. In an effort to _____ any problems with the new policies, we held a meeting so people could voice their concerns.

____ 4. The cacao tree is _____ to the New World, but cocoa and chocolate have become loved by the whole world.

____ 5. I consider myself _____; I love hamburgers and chicken, as well as fruits and vegetables.

SET 2

          a. zoology   b. moratorium   c. habitat   d. mammals   e. encroachment

____ 6. The continuous _____ on forests around the world endangers many plants that may provide cures for today's diseases.

____ 7. The _____ found in Africa, such as the elephant, are some of the largest in the world.

____ 8. Many creatures have adapted to a desert _____, and they have no problem living in extreme temperatures.

____ 9. Some aspects of _____ attract me, but I'm not sure I'm that interested in animals to spend years studying them.

____ 10. After I counted 100 pairs of shoes in my closet, I put a _____ on any more shoe shopping.

Name _____   Class _____   Date _____

Chapter 13—Quiz 1

Pick the vocabulary word that best completes the sentence.

___ 1. I was too _____ with my studying, so I wasn't prepared for the first exam.
    a. credibility   b. ordeal   c. lax   d. decipher

___ 2. The jeweler's _____ was in danger when he said the necklace was made of diamonds and it turned out to be made of glass.
    a. ordeal   b. credibility   c. adage   d. circumspection

___ 3. I sent my friend a postcard, but he couldn't _____ my cramped writing.
    a. decipher   b. defraud   c. spam   d. lax

___ 4. It was with _____ that I set out to discover who had broken my living room window. I carefully asked the neighbors what they had been doing last night.
    a. credibility   b. phishing   c. validity   d. circumspection

___ 5. The _____, "Look before you leap," is one I need to remember. I am always jumping into a project before I know enough about it.
    a. credibility   b. adage   c. ordeal   d. circumspection

___ 6. The man at the shop tried to _____ me. He said the vase had been made by a local artist, but I turned it over to look at the bottom and saw a "Made in China" sticker.
    a. defraud   b. decipher   c. lax   d. spam

___ 7. Writing this term paper has turned out to be a(n) _____. I faced one problem after another—from lost books in the library to a computer crash.
    a. adage   b. ordeal   c. phishing   d. validity

___ 8. I have been getting less _____ in my inbox since I accept e-mail only from people on my safe list.
    a. validity   b. circumspection   c. spam   d. adages

___ 9. The _____ of the contract was called into question when it was discovered that Mrs. Archer's signature had been forged by her eldest son.
    a. ordeal   b. adage   c. circumspection   d. validity

___ 10. I think someone is _____ for my personal information. When I went to a site that looked like my bank, I was asked to give my social security number.
    a. spam   b. validity   c. phishing   d. deciphering

Name _____   Class _____   Date _____

Chapter 13—Quiz 2

For each set, pick the vocabulary word that best completes the sentence. Use each word once.

SET 1

       a. adage   b. lax   c. ordeal   d. defraud   e. validity

____ 1. Shopping with my sister is such a(n) _____. She can never make up her
      mind, so we often have to go back to the same store several times.

____ 2. My friend's favorite _____ is "We'll cross that bridge when we come to
      it." I, on the other hand, am always thinking about what might happen, and she tells
      me that I worry too much.

____ 3. My friend was _____ about installing security on his computer, and he got a
      virus on it.

____ 4. I doubt the _____ of most statements Sam makes; I have checked
      several of his claims and found them to be untrue.

____ 5. It was a shock when Gregory was caught trying to _____ a customer.
      He was considered one of the most honest store owners in our community.

SET 2

       a. spam   b. phishing   c. decipher   d. credibility   e. circumspection

____ 6. Tammy's _____ disappeared when it was disclosed that she had been selling
      phony baseball cards.

____ 7. I couldn't _____ my teacher's comments, so I went to her office to ask what she
      had written. She appreciated my effort to understand her writing.

____ 8. I won't buy anything from a company that thinks it is all right to _____
      people. I don't consider that to be an acceptable use of e-mail.

____ 9. I should have used more _____ to find out who had used my stapler and
      tape. Some of my co-workers became angry when I asked about their using them.

____ 10. I got an e-mail today that appeared to be from my credit-card company, but
      when I went to the site, I suspected someone was _____ because I was
      asked for several pieces of personal information.

Name _____   Class _____   Date _____

Chapter 14—Quiz 1

Pick the vocabulary word that best completes the sentence.

___ 1. Several government agencies use _____, such as FBI for Federal Bureau of
Investigation.
a. homonyms   b. euphemisms   c. colloquialisms   d. acronyms

___ 2. I wanted a(n) _____ answer, not a 20-minute response.
a. cliché   b. scrutinize   c. concise   d. acronym

___ 3. I gave such an enthusiastic _____ of the movie that several people in my
class went to see it that night.

a. homonym   b. colloquialism   c. irony   d. synopsis

___ 4. My cousin's actions often _____ me. Why would she buy ten new plants and the
next week leave on a trip for two months and not ask anyone to take care of them?

a. concise   b. bewilder   c. scrutinize   d. synopsis

___ 5. There was a definite _____ in my being caught in the rain without my umbrella
when every morning I ask my husband, "Did you remember your umbrella?"
a. irony   b. cliché   c. concise   d. acronym

Finish the story using the vocabulary words. Use each word once.

a. cliché   b. euphemism   c. scrutinize   d. homonyms   e. colloquialism

I like to (6.)_____ the Sunday paper looking for examples of terms I have recently

learned in my courses. This week I found several examples related to words I have learned in

my English class. On the weather page, I found a(n) (7.)_____ in a story reporting

that tomorrow it would be "raining cats and dogs." On the sports page, a headline used the

(8.)_____ "Goin'" to announce the departure of our basketball team to another city. In

the classified section, someone had a "saleboat for sail." That person clearly needs a lesson in

(9.)_____. Finally, in the real estate section, a house was described as a "charming fixer,"

which I saw as an obvious (10.)_____ for a rundown shack.

___ 6.   ___ 7.   ___ 8.   ___ 9.   ___ 10.

40

Name _____ Class _____ Date _____

Chapter 14—Quiz 2

For each set, pick the vocabulary word that best completes the sentence. Use each word once.

SET 1

     a. bewildered   b. concise   c. acronyms   d. irony   e. synopsis

____ 1. My _____ of the novel was supposed to be no longer than one page, but it was difficult to sum up all that happened in so short a space.

____ 2. The test instructions said to give _____ answers for each question. I guess that's why there were only two lines on which to write.

____ 3. I bought a book with _____ to decode. Some were common, such as ASAP, but others I had never heard of, such as TCB.

____ 4. The detective in the movie I watched last night was _____ by a key that was found in the suspect's purse, but didn't fit her door. He finally figured out that two keys had been switched.

____ 5. It took me awhile to appreciate the _____ of my big date with Mike. I pictured him taking me to a fancy restaurant and us strolling along the beach hand in hand after dinner. In reality, he took me out for ice cream and challenged me to a running race afterwards.

SET 2

     a. colloquialism   b. euphemisms   c. scrutinize   d. homonyms   e. cliché

____ 6. The _____ *patience* and *patients* are both important to the medical field.

____ 7. After I got sick, my mother said I looked as white as a ghost. I thought the _____ was too strong, but when I looked in the mirror, I saw she was right.

____ 8. I decided that it would be inappropriate to begin my letter with "Howdy." The _____ was much too informal for the company to which I was applying.

____ 9. I felt I should _____ the rental contract before I signed it. I didn't want to be surprised by any unusual rules after I moved into the apartment.

____ 10. My friends and I thought the man's behavior was rude, but his wife used the words "gruff" and "challenging" to describe his manners, which we saw as _____.

41

Chapter 15—Quiz 1

Match the word part to its meaning. Use the sample words to help you make the connections.

Prefixes

____ 1. am- (amiable, amateur)

____ 2. eu- (euphoria, eulogy)

____ 3. pan- (pandemonium, panorama)

Roots

____ 4. -don-, -dot-, -dow- (donate, endow)

____ 5. -fer- (transfer, confer)

____ 6. -mis-, -mit- (mission, transmit)

____ 7. -ven-, -vent- (convene, circumvent)

Suffixes

____ 8. -ia (hysteria, nostalgia)

____ 9. -il, -ile (virile, agile)

____ 10. -sis (synopsis, hypothesis)

a. all, everywhere	ab. condition
b. love	ac. good, well
c. process or state	ad. to send
d. to give	ae. to bring, to carry
e. pertaining to or able	bc. to come, to move toward

Name_____ Class_____ Date_____

Chapter 15—Quiz 2

Match the word part to its meaning. Use the sample words to help you make the connections.

Prefixes

____ 1. eu- (euphoria, euphemistic)

____ 2. am- (amiable, amorous)

____ 3. pan- (pandemonium, panorama)

Roots

____ 4. -fer- (fertile, confer)

____ 5. -don-, -dot-, -dow- (antidote, endow)

____ 6. -mis-, -mit- (emissary, intermittent)

____ 7. -ven-, -vent- (intervene, event)

Suffixes

____ 8. -il, -ile (fragile, virile)

____ 9. -ia (hysteria, euphoria)

____ 10. -sis (synopsis, catharsis)

a. process or state   ab. condition
b. love   ac. good, well
c. all, everywhere   ad. to send
d. to give   ae. to bring, to carry
e. pertaining to or able   bc. to come, to move toward

43

Name _____   Class _____   Date _____

Chapter 16—Quiz 1

Pick the vocabulary word that best completes the sentence.

___ 1. I wanted to _____ my nephew's interest in science, so I bought him a
      telescope.
      a. defraud   b. nurture   c. decipher   d. bewilder

___ 2. I tend to get more _____ over the weekend, so I spend Monday morning
      cleaning out my e-mail messages.
      a. irony   b. moratorium   c. encroachment   d. spam

___ 3. The _____ gave an interesting talk on the native plants found in the park and what
      was being done to preserve them.
      a. spam   b. advocate   c. conservationist   d. euphemism

___ 4. I confused my cooking class with my _____ error. My recipe noted to add *flower*
      instead of *flour*. People asked if a rose or a violet would work better.
      a. phishing   b. habitat   c. potential   d. homonym

___ 5. My parents are strong _____ of letting children pick their own hobbies.
      a. advocates   b. mammals   c. homonyms   d. adages

___ 6. I am most impressed with large _____ like elephants and tigers.
      a. homonyms   b. ordeals   c. advocates   d. mammals

___ 7. Josh's _____ was hurt when he lied to me about where he had been all weekend.
      a. credibility   b. irony   c. potential   d. encroachment

___ 8. After driving for twenty hours, I could honestly use the _____ "sleep like a log"
      to describe how I felt.
      a. nurture   b. zoology   c. cliché   d. circumspection

___ 9. I loved the _____ in the story when the man decided to marrying the woman
      he thought was poor, and she turned out to be richer than the woman he had been dating.
      a. irony   b. spam   c. nurture   d. conservationist

___ 10. The polar bears' _____ is endangered by global warming.
      a. ordeal   b. advocate   c. habitat   d. acronym

For each set, pick the vocabulary word that best completes the sentence.

a. endemic   b. concise   c. lax   d. innate   e. susceptible

____ 11. I am _____ to ads dealing with food, so I close my eyes when they come on.
____ 12. One of June's _____ qualities is her ability to listen to others' problems.
____ 13. I have been _____ about eating healthy; I need to change my ways.
____ 14. These flowers are _____ to the southwestern part of the United States.
____ 15. I enjoy reading the _____ accounts of the city council meetings in the local paper.

a. defraud   b. avert   c. facilitate   d. impede   e. bewilders

____ 16. I don't let my job _____ my education; I can balance work and school.
____ 17. It always _____ me how quickly the weekend disappears.
____ 18. I was happy to _____ at the registration table. I like meeting new people.
____ 19. I don't buy things from people who call me. I am afraid that they are trying to _____ me.
____ 20. To _____ last month's problem of having all desserts at the potluck, we will assign people a category based on last names.

Match the word to its definition.

____ 21. adage   a. to examine carefully
____ 22. impose   b. to draw or bring out
____ 23. elicit   c. a traditional saying
____ 24. scrutinize   d. watchfulness; caution
____ 25. circumspection   e. to force on others

Finish the story using the vocabulary words. Use each word once.

a. validity   b. ordeal   c. euphemism   d. adhere   e. moratorium

When I was sixteen, my parents put a two-week (26.)_____ on my using the computer. They said I was spending too much time on it. I said I was simply being "attentive." They said that was just a(n) (27.)_____ for being obsessed by it. There was some (28.)_____ to their point. I often spent ten hours a day on the computer. I agreed to (29.)_____ to their decision. The first week it was quite the (30.)_____ to stay off the computer. But soon I realized I had needed to get out more. I was now ready to use the computer more wisely.

____ 26.   ____ 27.   ____ 28.   ____ 29.   ____ 30.

Use the words below to help you match the word part to its meaning.

____ 31. eu-: euphoria, eulogy, euphemism   a. condition
____ 32. -fer-: transfer, offer, conference   b. good, well
____ 33. -il,ile: virile, versatile, fragile   c. to give
____ 34. -don-, -dot-, -dow-: donate, antidote, donor   d. to bring, to carry
____ 35. -ia: hysteria, insomnia, euphoria   e. pertaining to or able

Name _____   Class _____   Date _____

Chapter 16—Quiz 2

Pick the vocabulary word that best completes the sentence.

___ 1. For my final _____ project, I have decided to study the behavior of camels.
    a. potential   b. zoology   c. euphemism   d. phishing

___ 2. Roberta rarely follows instructions at school. Her mother uses the term "forceful" to describe her behavior, but most of her teachers see that as a _____ for "stubborn."
    a. nurture   b. credibility   c. euphemism   d. habitat

___ 3. I am a(n) _____ eater; I enjoy fresh fruits and juicy hamburgers.
    a. innate   b. omnivorous   c. lax   d. concise

___ 4. After six cell phones rang in class last week, my teacher _____ a cell-phone ban.
    a. defrauded   b. bewildered   c. elicited   d. imposed

___ 5. I suspected a _____ scheme when the Web site asked for my mother's maiden name and my e-mail password to confirm that a credit card belonged to me.
    a. habitat   b. homonym   c. phishing   d. nurturing

___ 6. I try not to use _____ during speech class because I want my presentations to be formal.
    a. advocates   b. ordeals   c. mammals   d. colloquialisms

___ 7. It is time for our supervisor to put a _____ on bringing pets to work. It feels more like a pet store than an office with all the dogs, cats, and rabbits here.
    a. potential   b. colloquialism   c. credibility   d. moratorium

___ 8. Helpfulness is _____ in Mark; he has been that way since birth.
    a. concise   b. innate   c. lax   d. omnivorous

___ 9. The police officer checked the _____ of the woman's driver's license when he stopped her for speeding. He found that it was fake.
    a. validity   b. irony   c. potential   d. zoology

___ 10. I have the _____ to do well in my tennis class if I practice on the weekends.
    a. lax   b. potential   c. concise   d. endemic

For each set, pick the vocabulary word that best completes the sentence.

    a. spam   b. decipher   c. elicit   d. surpass   e. scrutinize

___ 11. After ten minutes of careful studying, I was able to _____ my brother's note.
___ 12. I want to _____ my family's expectations, so I am going to study extra hard.
___ 13. I didn't mean to _____ my contacts with the e-mail to my sister. I don't know how I
        sent it to so many people.
___ 14. I need to _____ Tom's reports since he has made five errors this week.
___ 15. I will _____ my friends' opinions before I decide what kind of car to buy.

    a. advocate   b. acronyms   c. circumspection   d. mammals   e. encroachment

___ 16. When I returned to my hometown after being gone for five years, I was shocked at the
        _____ of the houses on the forest
___ 17. I will use _____ to find out what gifts people want this holiday season.
___ 18. I like to use _____ when I e-mail my friends because it saves me typing time.
___ 19. I am a strong _____ for cleaner rivers and oceans.
___ 20. I have joined a group to protect the _____ and reptiles in the nearby desert.

Match the word to its definition.

___ 21. bewilder   a. a summary
___ 22. habitat   b. to cheat
___ 23. defraud   c. to follow closely or to stick together
___ 24. synopsis   d. to confuse, baffle, or puzzle
___ 25. adhere   e. surroundings

Finish the story using the vocabulary words. Use each word once.
    a. ordeal   b. facilitate   c. irony   d. concise   e. avert

I was happy to (26.)_____ with the fund raiser. Some people consider it an unbearable
(27.)_____ to plan a rummage sale, but I didn't find it that difficult. To (28.)_____
any major problems, I gathered a group of dedicated volunteers to help me on the day of the sale.
I told them to be friendly, but (29.)_____ with people when they worked the cash register
and that would help the line move quickly. The biggest (30.)_____ about my helping
with the event is that I couldn't donate anything to the sale because I am such a saver.
    ___ 26.   ___ 27.   ___ 28.   ___ 29.   ___ 30.

Use the words below to help you match the word part to its meaning.

___ 31. -mis-, -mit-: transmit, mission, intermittent   a. all, everywhere
___ 32. am-: amiable, amateur, amorous   b. to send
___ 33. -ven-, -vent-: convene, circumvent, intervene   c. process or state
___ 34. -sis: synopsis, hypothesis, catharsis   d. love
___ 35. pan-: pandemonium, panoramic, pantheon   e. to come, to move toward

47

Name _____   Class _____   Date _____

Chapter 17—Quiz 1

Pick the vocabulary word that best completes the sentence.

___ 1. The mayor agreed to _____ the building a city landmark after 20,000
        people signed a petition requesting the special designation.
        a. plunder   b. secular   c. plague   d. proclaim

___ 2. _____ was a system that created a strong class structure.
        a. Homage   b. Feudalism   c. Plunder   d. Alliance

___ 3. The _____ struck the village hard. Almost half of the population was
        killed.
        a. plague   b. medieval   c. alliance   d. secular

___ 4. My daughter's track team knows how to _____ a kitchen; there wasn't
        much food left when I came in for a snack.
        a. alliance   b. privilege   c. plunder   d. proclaim

___ 5. Alfonso thinks I am a(n) _____ because I don't like opera.
        a. feudalism   b. barbarian   c. homage   d. privilege

Match the word to its definition.

___ 6. homage   a. an agreement to cooperate

___ 7. secular   b. an advantage

___ 8. medieval   c. honor; tribute

___ 9. alliance   d. worldly

___ 10. privilege   e. of the Middle Ages

Name _____   Class _____   Date _____

Chapter 17—Quiz 2

For each set, pick the vocabulary word that best completes the sentence. Use each word once.

SET 1

         a. privilege   b. homage   c. alliances   d. plundered   e. plague

____ 1. Freedom of speech is a(n) _____ that people in some countries do not have.

____ 2. During a war, making the right _____ can lead to victory.

____ 3. The artist says her painting is a(n) _____ to Picasso, which is easy to see in her use of unusual angles.

____ 4. If the flies continue to _____ us, we will have to move our picnic inside.

____ 5. Many of the art collections of Europe were _____ during World War II.

SET 2

         a. medieval   b. proclaimed c. secular   d. barbarian   e. feudalism

____ 6. He was a(n) _____ when it came to eating. I rarely saw Conrad use a knife or fork.

____ 7. Castles are among the treasures constructed in Europe during _____ times.

____ 8. Frieda _____ her innocence, but the police still brought her in for questioning.

____ 9. My interests have always been in _____ areas. I love business, gossip, and a good game of poker.

____ 10. _____ isn't likely to gain popularity in this century; most people want to own at least a parcel of their own land.

Name _____   Class _____   Date _____

Chapter 18—Quiz 1

Pick the vocabulary word that best completes the sentence.

____ 1. The weather forecaster predicted _____ showers, so I took my umbrella in order to be prepared.
   a. fertile   b. Renaissance   c. intermittent   d. façade

____ 2. I had the _____ to pack a lunch for the conference because I thought the nearby restaurants might be closed on a Monday.
   a. cupola   b. humanism   c. fresco   d. foresight

____ 3. The lion statues made the _____ of the building look stately.
   a. façade   b. Renaissance   c. fresco   d. humanism

____ 4. The _____ was a time of great achievements in the arts.
   a. humanism   b. Renaissance   c. cupola   d. foresight

____ 5. The article proved to be a(n) _____ source of ideas for topics for future essays.
   a. fresco   b. fertile   c. intermittent   d. endowed

____ 6. The _____ on the church walls still looked surprisingly fresh even though they were painted more than five hundred years ago.
   a. façades   b. frescos   c. cupolas   d. adorns

____ 7. I could see the _____ on the state capitol when I was six blocks away.
   a. foresight   b. fresco   c. humanism   d. cupola

____ 8. Alicia is _____ with many talents from acting to writing.
   a. endowed   b. adorned   c. fertile   d. intermittent

____ 9. The classroom was _____ with the children's artwork.
   a. endowed   b. adorned   c. fertile   d. intermittent

____ 10. The rise of _____ led to changes in art and architecture during the Renaissance.
   a. humanism   b. foresight   c. cupola   d. fresco

Name _____ Class _____ Date _____

Chapter 18—Quiz 2

For each set, pick the vocabulary word that best completes the sentence. Use each word once.

SET 1

       a. fertile   b. fresco   c. humanism d. endow   e. adorned

____ 1. Posters of famous athletes _____ the boy's room.

____ 2. The land proved to be _____. Corn and potatoes were a few of the crops that grew abundantly.

____ 3. A renewed interest in learning and _____ are two qualities of the Renaissance.

____ 4. The _____ was badly damaged when a bomb hit the church.

____ 5. We were so excited when the Young Foundation said it was going to _____ the museum with a million dollars.

SET 2

       a. foresight   b. intermittent   c. Renaissance   d. façade   e. cupola

____ 6. When the hotel owners reported that, to attract attention, they were going to paint the _____ bright orange, several people in the community were upset.

____ 7. Andrew displayed a calm _____ when his girlfriend said she wanted to break up, but inside he was miserable.

____ 8. If we have the _____ to protect nature, future generations will be able to enjoy the beauties of the oceans, forests, and deserts.

____ 9. The _____ announcements at the airport made it hard to concentrate on my book.

____ 10. Rome has several reminders of the great achievements of the _____.

Name _____   Class _____   Date _____

Chapter 19—Quiz 1

Pick the vocabulary word that best completes the sentence.

____ 1. His _____ class reunion finally got Mark to start exercising and eating right. He
        wanted to lose twenty pounds in the next two months.
        a. wrest   b. infrastructure   c. impending   d. figurehead

____ 2. When it was time to go to bed, I had to _____ the lollipop out of my son's hands. He
        wanted to sleep with it, but I was afraid it would have ended up stuck in his hair.
        a. figurehead b. wrest   c. depose   d. coup

____ 3. Winning the trip to Europe didn't seem in the _____ of possibility, but we entered
        the contest anyways.
        a. charisma   b. coup   c. regime   d. realm

____ 4. When his ten-year-old nephew became king, the evil uncle dreamt of a way to
        _____ him.
        a. depose   b. wrest   c. zenith   d. realm

____ 5. The company reached its _____ when it opened its eight-hundredth store. Three
        years later, bad management led to selling off several stores.
        a. realm   b. charisma   c. zenith   d. coup

Finish the story using the vocabulary words. Use each word once.

      a. charisma   b. coup   c. figurehead   d. infrastructure   e. regime

The country's (6.)_____ was crumbling because the dictator spent the tax money on

airplanes, fancy homes, and other luxuries for himself and the upper class. It was only after the

(7.)_____ that many of the upper class realized how bad the country's problems had

become. The new (8.)_____ was supposedly in the hands of General Faustus. He had

(9.)_____, but he lacked the intelligence to really run the country. He was merely

a(n)(10.) _____. The real person in power was Alexandra Lopez, the owner of the

newspaper. In her paper, she had promised to help the poor and rebuild the country.

    ____ 6.   ____ 7.   ____ 8.   ____ 9.   ____ 10.

Name _____ Class _____ Date _____

Chapter 19—Quiz 2

For each set, pick the vocabulary word that best completes the sentence. Use each word once.

SET 1

     a. coup   b. impending c. regime   d. depose   e. infrastructure

___ 1. Queen Victoria's _____ was one of the longest in British history.

___ 2. When Adele cleaned her office, rumors began to circulate of her _____ firing.

___ 3. The company's _____ was shaken when its founder died; no one had his vision.

___ 4. After the club's executive directors planned a third expensive retreat in the mountains in one year, the angry members organized a plan to _____ them.

___ 5. The _____ was supposed to install a democratic form of government, but soon the power was again in the hands of one person.

SET 2

     a. charisma b. realm   c. figurehead d. zenith   e. wrest

___ 6. Sumiko was only a _____ during her tenure as president; the vice-president made all the important decisions.

___ 7. The _____ of the governor's time in office came when he was able to announce that the state was no longer in debt and that it even had a surplus of funds for emergencies.

___ 8. Jose decided to explore the _____ of cooking. He had always thought he had the potential to be a great chef.

___ 9. Velma's _____ attracted many people to her campaign for mayor.

___ 10. A group of concerned citizens gathered to develop a plan to _____ control of the library from the evil librarian.

Name _____   Class _____   Date _____

Chapter 20—Quiz 1

Pick the vocabulary word that best completes the sentence.

___ 1. My problems always seem to _____ at the end of the semester because I'm
    under a lot of stress then.
    a. asset   b. modify   c. venture   d. proliferate

___ 2. After much searching, Rosemary found her _____ in the company. She is
    perfect for the accounting department.
    a. asset   b. niche   c. liability   d. propensity

___ 3. My grandfather had to _____ his eating habits after he had a heart attack.
    He cut down on beef and salt.
    a. modify   b. venture   c. proliferate   d. entrepreneur

___ 4. I have a(n) _____ to date tall women, but I'm not sure why I have such a
    preference.
    a. venture   b. liability   c. entrepreneur   d. propensity

___ 5. Joseph's latest business _____ combines travel and sports. He is
    enthusiastic about both areas, so it might work out quite well for him.
    a. jovial   b. venture   c. asset   d. entrepreneur

___ 6. Even though I displayed the photograph in a(n) _____ place, no one at the
    party commented on it. I was surprised because I thought it was one of my best
    shots.
    a. prominent   b. jovial   c. modified   d. proliferate

___ 7. Isaac is a _____ man. He loves to tell jokes, and he enjoys a good laugh.
    a. proliferate   b. jovial   c. prominent   d. entrepreneur

___ 8. I borrowed money from a friend, and now the loan has become a(n) _____ in
    that relationship. I need to show Edith that I am a responsible person by paying
    her back soon.
    a. asset   b. niche   c. liability   d. entrepreneur

___ 9. One of the _____ of living in a big city is having several activities to choose
    from, such as museums, concerts, and sporting events.
    a. liabilities   b. niches   c. assets   d. ventures

___ 10. My friend said I would make a good _____ because I am friendly, I like to
    work hard, and I have innovative ideas. She convinced me to start my own company.
    a. propensity   b. venture   c. liability   d. entrepreneur

54

Name _____   Class _____   Date _____

Chapter 20—Quiz 2

For each set, pick the vocabulary word that best completes the sentence. Use each word once.

SET 1

      a. propensity   b. niche   c. asset   d. liability   e. entrepreneur

____ 1. The _____ gave a fascinating talk on the rewards and the problems of starting one's own business.

____ 2. My sense of humor is often the _____ that gets me through a busy day at work.

____ 3. Jed has become a(n) _____ to the project; he keeps making inappropriate comments that insult our clients.

____ 4. The figurine will be perfect in the _____ underneath the stairs.

____ 5. Lily's _____ for eating chocolate had serious consequences: the dentist found three cavities during Lily's last visit.

SET 2

      a. jovial   b. prominent   c. venture   d. modify   e. proliferate

____ 6. I enjoyed the _____ atmosphere at the campout. It was a pleasurable way to spend a weekend.

____ 7. The junk in the attic continues to _____ though no one claims to put anything up there.

____ 8. I will _____ a guess as to why Lee is late, but I can't be certain of the reason.

____ 9. Jessica is a _____ citizen. She has donated a large sum toward building the new library, and she is on the board of several community organizations.

____ 10. We had to _____ our route after the storm washed out the bridge.

Name _____   Class _____   Date _____

Chapter 21—Quiz 1

Pick the vocabulary word that best completes the sentence.

____ 1. I plan to _____ my front room with lots of plants and flowers once spring comes
around.
a. proliferate   b. adorn   c. depose   d. homage

____ 2. I think my greatest _____ is my ability to save. I will always have money set
aside in case of an emergency.
a. asset   b. humanism   c. liability   d. infrastructure

____ 3. The woman's _____ helped her greatly in politics. She went from being a mayor
to governor to senator in six years.
a. privilege   b. cupola   c. charisma   d. entrepreneur

____ 4. I have a _____ to put off studying until the night before a test; I would feel
better and learn more if I studied over weeks instead of hours.
a. foresight   b. plague   c. privilege   d. propensity

____ 5. When the committee told Marshall that the president was only a _____, he resigned
from the position. He really wanted to do something to help the organization.
a. fresco   b. barbarian   c. figurehead   d. niche

____ 6. Thanks to the founder's _____, the college can continue to grow. In his
will he bestowed several parcels of nearby land to the college.
a. niche   b. alliance   c. foresight   d. charisma

____ 7. I am afraid this cold is going to _____ me for another week.
a. plague   b. endow   c. depose   d. modify

____ 8. I have several characteristics of a good _____, so I am going to start my own
business.
a. barbarian   b. renaissance   c. entrepreneur   d. realm

____ 9. Life during the _____ period doesn't appeal to me at all.
a. jovial   b. medieval   c. fertile   d. impending

____ 10. The people banded together to _____ the cruel king.
a. depose   b. endow   c. proclaim   d. venture

For each set, pick the vocabulary word that best completes the sentence.

  a. secular b. jovial c. impending d. fertile e. intermittent

___ 11. There was lots of laughter at the party. We were a(n) _____ group.
___ 12. The fields were so _____ that we had plenty of food to feed the whole village.
___ 13. The monk was unhappy at the monastery, so he decided to rejoin the _____ world.
___ 14. The _____ wedding was making the bride nervous. She still had so much to do.
___ 15. The forecast calls for _____ snow showers for the next two weeks. I will get my
   groceries in between the storms.

  a. infrastructure b. feudalism c. liability d. humanism e. homage

___ 16. _____ created a hard life for the serfs, while the nobles prospered.
___ 17. The dance recital was a(n) _____ to Martha Graham's work.
___ 18. Missing deadlines is Patricia's greatest _____.
___ 19. _____ helped to focus the arts on the values and concerns of people.
___ 20. The _____ of the company was strengthened when Amelia was hired; her
   organizational skills helped stabilize the firm.

Match the word to its definition.

___ 21. renaissance a. painting done on moist plaster
___ 22. plunder   b. to grow
___ 23. proliferate   c. a rebirth; a revival
___ 24. fresco   d. overthrow of the government
___ 25. coup   e. to raid

Finish the story using the vocabulary words. Use each word once.
  a. façade b. zenith c. proclaim d. prominent e. privileges

Jason said he came from a (26.)_____ family in Boston. He told me that he grew up
enjoying several (27.)_____ because his family was so well known. He mentioned that the
(28.)_____ of his life so far was assisting doctors in Africa. I was impressed. Then I found
out that everything he had told me about himself was part of a (29.)_____. He really came
from a middle-class family in Omaha, and he had never been to Africa. I enjoyed his company,
so I was disappointed that he felt he had to (30.)_____ himself to be someone he wasn't.
 ___ 26. ___ 27. ___ 28. ___ 29. ___ 30.

Use the words below to help you match the word part to its meaning.

___ 31. anti-: antipathy, antidote, antisocial   a. to bring; to carry
___ 32. -ism: feudalism, patriotism, humanism   b. against
___ 33. -fer-: proliferate, fertile, transfer   c. to hang; to weigh; to pay
___ 34. -pend-, -pens-: impending, suspend, propensity d. to shout; to call out
___ 35. -claim-: proclaim, exclaim, reclaim   e. action; practice, theory

Name _____   Class _____   Date _____

Chapter 21—Quiz 2

Pick the vocabulary word that best completes the sentence.

___ 1. Because my work on the back yard was only _____, it took a long time to finish the flower garden.
    a. fertile   b. medieval   c. impending   d. intermittent

___ 2. The _____ was so oppressive that people were eager to revolt.
    a. regime   b. propensity   c. Renaissance   d. privilege

___ 3. The pirates came to _____ the riches of the plantations in the Caribbean.
    a. plunder   b. adorn   c. depose   d. modify

___ 4. The _____ of the building is undergoing repairs.
    a. figurehead   b. plague   c. venture   d. façade

___ 5. The _____ meeting at work has several people worried. They think cut backs are going to be announced.
    a. secular   b. fertile   c. impending   d. prominent

___ 6. The king _____ his birthday a holiday.
    a. wrested   b. endowed   c. ventured   d. proclaimed

___ 7. The _____ was a grand success. The people were finally rid of the dictator.
    a. coup   b. asset   c. plague   d. fresco

___ 8. Francie is a _____ woman in the community. She owns her own business, is a member of the city council, and assists several charitable organizations.
    a. jovial   b. prominent   c. medieval   d. intermittent

___ 9. The city's _____ is in good shape after six years of widespread repairs.
    a. alliance   b. humanism   c. infrastructure   d. entrepreneur

___ 10. The statue fit perfectly in the _____ and attracted several compliments.
    a. coup   b. niche   c. foresight   d. barbarian

For each set, pick the vocabulary word that best completes the sentence.

a. adorned   b. modify   c. plague   d. depose   e. proliferate

____ 11. The board had to _____ the president after he stole money from the company.
____ 12. Because I am so stressed, my health problems continue to _____.
____ 13. I have to _____ our meeting plans since I will be an hour late.
____ 14. The room was _____ with balloons and hearts for the Valentine party.
____ 15. The pain in my knee continues to _____ me since I slipped on the ice last month.

a. realm   b. cupola   c. alliance   d. entrepreneur   e. barbarians

____ 16. I want to be a(n) _____ some day. I would love to be my own boss.
____ 17. The drama and music departments formed a(n) _____ to promote the Arts Festival.
____ 18. The _____ on the bank broke off during the tornado.
____ 19. I have always been interested in the _____ of science, so I am taking classes in chemistry and astronomy this semester.
____ 20. When the _____ invaded the town, everyone hid.

Match the word to its definition.

____ 21. proclaim   a. the highest point
____ 22. fertile   b. merry; good-humored
____ 23. jovial   c. concern for the future
____ 24. zenith   d. to state publicly
____ 25. foresight   e. very productive

Finish the story using the vocabulary words. Use each word once.
a. privilege   b. endowed   c. asset   d. venture   e. charisma

I couldn't turn Carlotta down when she asked for my help at the college luncheon. She has so much (26.) _____ that I can never refuse her requests. She is a major (27.) _____ to any group because she can always get volunteers. When she asked if I could spend the whole day at the event, I said, "It would be a (28.) _____ to devote my day to such a good cause." I would (29.) _____ to say that without Carlotta's efforts the school would not run as smoothly. Carlotta is (30.) _____ with several good qualities including generosity.

____ 26.   ____ 27.   ____ 28.   ____ 29.   ____ 30.

Use the words below to help you match the word part to its meaning.

____ 31. -ify: modify, clarify, magnify   a. to send
____ 32. -fer-: proliferate, fertile, transfer   b. to bring; to carry
____ 33. -mis-, -mit-: submissive, emissary, intermittent   c. wrong
____ 34. mis-: misgiving, miscalculation, mistake   d. to make
____ 35. -pend-, -pens-: impending, spend, propensity   e. to hang, to weigh, to pay

59

Name _____   Class _____   Date _____

Chapter 22—Quiz 1

Pick the vocabulary word that best completes the sentence.

____ 1. I like the way Alexa furnished her house; she used a(n) _____ blend of
pieces ranging from French traditional to American Southwest.
a. holistic   b. unparalleled   c. eclectic   d. naturopathic

____ 2. The cat considers the sun room her _____ and chases the dog out whenever he
tries to enter.
a. domain   b. syndrome   c. deficiency   d. antidote

____ 3. My grandmother is an example of _____: she turned 110 last week.
a. anemia   b. longevity   c. deficiency   d. syndromes

____ 4. There is a(n) _____ of desks at the college, so some people are going to
have to stand for a few weeks until the new desks arrive.
a. syndrome   b. longevity   c. antidote   d. deficiency

____ 5. I like the _____ approach to medicine; I want my body to be examined
in its entirety.
a. eclectic   b. holistic   c. unparalleled   d. deficiency

____ 6. I am using a(n) _____ treatment based on exercise and eating habits.
a. anemic   b. unparalleled   c. domain   d. naturopathic

____ 7. The service at the Hotel Wondermont was _____. I have never been waited
on so efficiently or courteously.
a. eclectic   b. naturopathic   c. unparalleled   d. holistic

____ 8. The _____ to my lack of interest in biology was a D on the first quiz. That
grade cured me of laziness.
a. longevity   b. antidote   c. anemia   d. deficiency

____ 9. I take iron pills to cope with my _____.
a. anemia   b. longevity   c. domain   d. naturopathic

____ 10. I told the doctor that some of my symptoms were a continuous cough, a rash on
my arm, and a loss of appetite. He said it sounded as if it might be a stress-related
_____.
a. deficiency   b. domain   c. syndrome   d. antidote

60

Name _____   Class _____   Date _____

Chapter 22—Quiz 2

For each set, pick the vocabulary word that best completes the sentence. Use each word once.

SET 1

     a. eclectic   b. anemia   c. longevity   d. naturopathic e. antidote

___ 1. I found the ultimate _____ to my exercise worries in a sport I love: bicycling.

___ 2. When I learned that I was suffering from _____, I was relieved to know why I was always tired.

___ 3. My favorite restaurant has a(n) _____ menu. Among the choices of foods offered are Chinese, Mexican, and Greek dishes.

___ 4. I get _____ raises at work after five and ten years of service.

___ 5. My doctor asked if I would be interested in a(n) _____ treatment instead of taking pills.

SET 2

     a. syndrome b. domain   c. holistic   d. unparalleled   e. deficiency

___ 6. I went to a doctor who specializes in _____ health care because I wanted to try some non-traditional treatments.

___ 7. My mother's meat loaf is _____. I have never tasted meat loaf as delicious as she makes.

___ 8. I am glad massage is included in the _____ of my new insurance program; I feel rejuvenated after a good massage.

___ 9. A(n) _____ of sleep was making me irritable. Now I try to get at least seven hours a night.

___ 10. Luckily, my _____ was treatable with exercise and changes to my eating patterns.

Name _____ Class _____ Date _____

Chapter 23—Quiz 1

Pick the vocabulary word that best completes the sentence.

____ 1. I enjoy eating dinner on my friend's penthouse patio because it has a(n) _____ view of the city and harbor below.
   a. panoramic   b. gateway   c. definitive   d. urban

____ 2. The new bank will be the largest _____ in town.
   a. gateway   b. panoramic   c. consensus   d. edifice

____ 3. Education is the _____ to a better future.
   a. panoramic   b. gateway   c. definitive   d. edifice

____ 4. The meeting will _____ at two o'clock and arguments for or against the plan will be heard before the voting takes place.
   a. endure   b. revitalize   c. rectify   d. convene

____ 5. I had to _____ another lecture on my poor exercise habits when my brother came home and found me sitting on the couch watching television for the fifth day in a row.
   a. endure   b. rectify   c. revitalize   d. convene

Match the word to its definition.

____ 6. revitalize   a. concerned with a city

____ 7. urban   b. to correct

____ 8. definitive   c. unity of opinion

____ 9. rectify   d. most reliable or complete

____ 10. consensus   e. to renew

62

Name _____   Class _____   Date _____

Chapter 23—Quiz 2

For each set, pick the vocabulary word that best completes the sentence. Use each word once.

SET 1

      a. endure   b. definitive   c. rectify   d. urban   e. revitalize

____ 1. To _____ the problem, I suggest you have an honest conversation with your friend.

____ 2. After several hours of discussion, the city council decided to _____ an area
      of abandoned warehouses south of town by creating a shopping and restaurant complex.

____ 3. I would like to give you a(n) _____ answer on whether we will make it for
      Thanksgiving dinner, but I still need to find out if I have to work the next day. If I do,
      a seven-hour drive is too far to travel for one day.

____ 4. I tried to like spinach, but the most I could _____ at first was a tablespoonful.

____ 5. I like _____ life. There is always something exciting to do in the city.

SET 2

      a. panoramic   b. gateway   c. edifice   d. consensus   e. convene

____ 6. Paris is a major _____ to Europe.

____ 7. I like to eat lunch on the hill near work because I can enjoy a(n) _____ view
      of the city while munching my sandwich.

____ 8. Reporters often _____ at the bottom of the courthouse steps to shout questions
      at attorneys involved in important cases.

____ 9. The group quickly reached a(n) _____ on where to go to lunch because
      everyone was hungry.

____ 10. The paper called the new jail a "monstrous _____," but I don't think the
      building looks that bad.

Name _____ Class _____ Date _____

Chapter 24—Quiz 1

Pick the vocabulary word that best completes the sentence.

____1. Her _____ with jewelry led to her spending more than she could afford on a
diamond necklace.
    a. ego   b. id   c. obsession   d. voyeurism

____2. The _____ use of products in the movie increased sales for those items
when the movie became a huge success.
    a. suppress   b. subliminal   c. amnesia   d. claustrophobia

____3. Because of Tom's _____, he said he could not remember why he charged
$10,000 in one weekend when he is usually very careful with how he spends his money.
    a. amnesia   b. voyeurism   c. claustrophobia   d. superego

____4. I had to _____ my urge to go swimming in the lake. It looked inviting, but
I had read in the newspaper that the water was possibly polluted.
    a. amnesia   b. subliminal   c. suppress   d. claustrophobia

____5. Marsha decided not to take the cave tour. She realized her _____ would make the
experience unpleasant for her.
    a. suppress   b. subliminal   c. amnesia   d. claustrophobia

Finish the story using the vocabulary words. Use each word once.

    a. superego   b. voyeurism   c. id   d. ego   e. hysteria

(6.)_____ can lead to interesting observations about one's neighbors. Lana noticed that

whenever it was hot her neighbor's (7.)_____ took over: Paul was angrier and ate and

drank to excess. During rainstorms, (8.)_____ was Paul's way of coping with the bad

weather. He would scream at the sky and laugh uncontrollably. When it was cold, Paul's

(9.)_____ took over. He would spend hours cleaning. And when it was pleasant, Paul's

(10.)_____ was in control, and he could safely be invited to dinner.

    ___ 6.   ___ 7.   ___ 8.   ___ 9.   ___ 10.

Name _____   Class _____   Date _____

Chapter 24—Quiz 2

For each set, pick the vocabulary word that best completes the sentence. Use each word once.

SET 1

      a. subliminal   b. claustrophobia   c. amnesia   d. obsession   e. suppress

____ 1. I thought about claiming _____ and missing the meeting, but it was supposed to be important, so I showed up along with 100 other employees.

____ 2. Unfortunately, the meeting room was small, and it was discovered that several employees suffer from _____ .

____ 3. I had to _____ a strong urge to leave myself; I certainly didn't want to stay in such a small space.

____ 4. Then I began to wonder if the company was sending a(n) _____ message about needing to downsize.

____ 5. Finally, a spokesperson told us that due to the company president's _____ for gambling, the company was broke, and we were all laid off.

SET 2

      a. id   b. superego   c. voyeurism   d. ego   e. hysteria

____ 6. John's _____ led to troubles with the police. His neighbors got tired of his peeking over their fences.

____ 7. Eve has to learn to control her _____ . She can't continue to yell at people when things don't go her way.

____ 8. When the winning goal was scored, the crowd's _____ was scary to see.

____ 9. Victor's _____ was hurt when he asked Millie for a date, and she turned him down.

___10. After Miranda learned to deal with her _____, she was much happier. She had too often been berating herself over small mistakes.

Name _____   Class _____   Date _____

Chapter 25—Quiz 1

Pick the vocabulary word that best completes the sentence.

____ 1. The book received _____ from all but one reviewer.
    a. acclaim   b. transcendent   c. subtle   d. pensive

____ 2. The actor stopped during his _____ because people in the front row were talking.
    a. catharsis   b. avant-garde   c. soliloquy   d. acclaim

____ 3. Gina made a(n) _____ change to the painting before exhibiting it. Most people won't notice the difference, but it has brightened the picture.
    a. pensive   b. avant-garde   c. subtle   d. transcendent

____ 4. The troop's _____ was "On with the show!" even when one cast member had a broken leg.
    a. finale   b. acclaim   c. pseudonym   d. credo

____ 5. The writer used a _____ when he wrote a review for his own book.
    a. catharsis   b. pseudonym   c. soliloquy   d. finale

____ 6. After seeing the play about the death of an old woman, the man experienced a _____ about the death of his grandmother.
    a. catharsis   b. pseudonym   c. soliloquy   d. finale

____ 7. The thought of appearing before thousands of people made the actor _____ before stepping onto the stage.
    a. subtle   b. pensive   c. avant-garde   d. finale

____ 8. The artwork was so _____ that it didn't even look like art. People thought it was a blanket that had been dropped on the ground.
    a. credo   b. pensive   c. avant-garde   d. transcendent

____ 9. The concert _____ caught everyone by surprise. The audience had so enjoyed the music that they didn't realize the show was ending.
    a. finale   b. soliloquy   c. credo   d. catharsis

____ 10. Donna's portrayal of Ophelia was _____. Never before had I seen anyone portray her pain with such feeling.
    a. pensive   b. transcendent   c. avant-garde   d. finale

Name _____   Class _____   Date _____

Chapter 25—Quiz 2

For each set, pick the vocabulary word that best completes the sentence. Use each word once.

SET 1

    a. transcendent   b. catharsis   c. pseudonym   d. pensive   e. avant-garde

____ 1. I was _____ about entering the writing contest.

____ 2. I thought I might write better if I used a(n) _____. I didn't want anyone to
        know I had written a story, just in case I lost the contest.

____ 3. My idea for the story was rather _____. The characters would be named
        after the planets and all the action would take place in a sewer.

____ 4. I found that writing the story was a(n) _____ for me. I was finally able to deal
        with some anger I had kept inside.

____ 5. You can imagine how _____ I felt when I won first place.

SET 2

    a. subtle   b. finale   c. credo   d. acclaim   e. soliloquy

____ 6. My _____ has always been to give everything a chance, so I went to the new
        play even though people said it wasn't very good.

____ 7. Before the first act ended, the main character gave a moving _____ on the
        meaning of his life.

____ 8. I appreciated the _____ ways the lighting changed to show a character's
        feelings.

____ 9. By the _____, I was impressed with the whole play.

____ 10. The play certainly deserved more _____ than it had been given.

Name _____   Class _____   Date _____

Chapter 26—Quiz 1

Pick the vocabulary word that best completes the sentence.

___ 1. The newest _____ downtown has been unfavorably compared to a giant curler, but I like its round shape.
    a. soliloquy   b. edifice   c. domain   d. hysteria

___ 2. Her outfit was a(n) _____ blend of seasons: shorts, a parka, and a rain hat.
    a. panoramic   b. transcendent   c. eclectic   d. subliminal

___ 3. The man quickly drank the _____ to stop the poison from spreading.
    a. edifice   b. catharsis   c. anemia   d. antidote

___ 4. The government tried to _____ the news about the uprising in the capitol, but the news spread from person to person.
    a. convene   b. acclaim   c. suppress   d. revitalize

___ 5. Because I couldn't _____ another burnt meal, I insisted on making dinner.
    a. endure   b. rectify   c. suppress   d. acclaim

___ 6. Because the waiter's service was _____, I left him an extra large tip.
    a. subliminal   b. pensive   c. panoramic   d. unparalleled

___ 7. My neighbor was accused of _____ by another neighbor, but it turns out that Freddie often wears binoculars because he is an avid bird-watcher.
    a. catharsis   b. voyeurism   c. anemia   d. consensus

___ 8. The movie opened to great _____, and it was later nominated for eight Academy awards.
    a. edifice   b. syndrome   c. voyeurism   d. acclaim

___ 9. I like the way Corrine _____ the old shed by turning it into an artist's studio.
    a. revitalized   b. convened   c. endured   d. suppressed

__ 10. The judge asked the lawyers to _____ in his chambers to discuss the case.
    a. endure   b. suppress   c. rectify   d. convene

For each set, pick the vocabulary word that best completes the sentence.

a. catharsis   b. gateway   c. soliloquy   d. anemia   e. claustrophobia

____ 11. The doctor discovered that her low energy was due to _____.
____ 12. Listening to Mozart provided the _____ I needed after a hard day at work.
____ 13. Sitting in the back seat of a compact car with four people exposed my _____ to the other passengers.
____ 14. The woman's _____ revealed how upset she was over the fight with her husband.
____ 15. The city constructed an impressive _____ for the new downtown shopping district.

a. subtle   b. urban   c. holistic   d. transcendent   e. subliminal

____ 16. I like my doctor's _____ approach to medicine.
____ 17. Living in a(n) _____ environment can be exciting, but also noisy.
____ 18. The magazine ads were filled with _____ messages to get people to buy more.
____ 19. I like the _____ taste of basil in the pasta sauce.
____ 20. The sets for the ballet were _____; the forest looked like a magical world.

Match the word to its definition.

____ 21. ego   a. lack; shortage
____ 22. deficiency   b. experimental
____ 23. superego   c. self-esteem
____ 24. avant-garde   d. thoughtful; reflective
____ 25. pensive   e. the moralistic part of a person

Finish the story using the vocabulary words. Use each word once.
a. rectify   b. credo   c. subliminal   d. domain   e. urban

The flier proclaimed, "Best massage in the city." I wondered if a massage might help to (26.)_____ some of the pain I have been having. Moving from the countryside to a busy (27.)_____ environment was causing quite a bit of stress in my life. I usually stay within the (28.)_____ of traditional medicine, but I was desperate for relief. Also I think there was a (29.)_____ message in the flier because I was mysteriously attracted to the place. After the massage, I felt fantastic! My new (30.)_____ is "anything is worth a try."

____ 26.   ____ 27.   ____ 28.   ____ 29.   ____ 30.

Use the words below to help you match the word part to its meaning.

____ 31. pan-: panoramic, pandemonium, panacea   a. condition
____ 32. -fin-: finale, definitive, finalist   b. all, everywhere
____ 33. -sub, sup-: subtle, subliminal, suppress   c. to believe; to trust
____ 34. -cred-: credo, credentials, credit   d. end; limit
____ 35. -ia: hysteria, insomnia, amnesia   e. below, under

69

Name _____   Class _____   Date _____

Chapter 26—Quiz 2

Pick the vocabulary word that best completes the sentence.

___ 1. My _____ was stroked when my friend said how much she liked my new hair cut.
    a. gateway   b. ego   c. syndrome   d. pseudonym

___ 2. The children could not come to a _____ on which miniature golf course to
    play, so half went to Storybook Land and half to Western World.
    a. soliloquy   b. consensus   c. gateway   d. superego

___ 3. I went to a(n) _____ doctor seeking relief for a pain in my foot that traditional
    treatments hadn't cured.
    a. holistic   b. subliminal   c. urban   d. pensive

___ 4. We wonder what caused Maude's _____. She can't remember where she went last
    week or what she did.
    a. amnesia   b. longevity   c. consensus   d. finale

___ 5. My grandmother's _____ is amazing; she turns 102 next week.
    a. catharsis   b. superego   c. edifice   d. longevity

___ 6. The _____ landscape is changing as more high rises are being built downtown.
    a. urban   b. subliminal   c. holistic   d. subtle

___ 7. I tried to _____ my feelings for Loretta, but I couldn't. When I told her
    how I felt, she said she was interested in me too.
    a. endure   b. revitalize   c. suppress   d. rectify

___ 8. I used a _____ when I signed up for an online dating service. I didn't want anyone to
    find out who I was right away.
    a. superego   b. deficiency   c. pseudonym   d. consensus

___ 9. After I tried an herb cure for my cough, I became interested in _____ medicine.
    a. panoramic   b. transcendent   c. pensive   d. naturopathic

___ 10. I was able to _____ the disagreement with my neighbor by inviting him to dinner
    and calmly discussing our differences.
    a. acclaim   b. suppress   c. convene   d. rectify

For each set, pick the vocabulary word that best completes the sentence.

a. subtle   b. unparalleled   c. avant-garde   d. subliminal   e. definitive

____ 11. The _____ exhibit featured artists working with crumbled pieces of paper.
____ 12. *Cookies, Cookies, and More Cookies* is the _____ cookbook for making cookies.
____ 13. The changes were _____, but they made the living room look bigger.
____ 14. The beauty of the snow-covered forest was _____. I have never seen anything more dazzling.
____ 15. I'm not sure I believe in _____ messages, but sometimes I do feel manipulated.

a. id   b. syndrome   c. edifice   d. obsession   e. soliloquy

____ 16. The hero's _____ explained why he was an angry man.
____ 17. I am suffering from some kind of _____, but the doctor's aren't sure what it is.
____ 18. My _____ for ice cream has led to midnight runs to the grocery.
____ 19. Sean let his _____ take over: all he did was eat and sleep all weekend.
____ 20. I like the newest _____ on campus. The music building looks quite grand.

Match the word to its definition.

____ 21. antidote   a. emotional excess
____ 22. domain   b. to applaud
____ 23. acclaim   c. scenic or pleasing
____ 24. hysteria   d. an area of concern; a field
____ 25. panoramic   e. a cure

Finish the story using the vocabulary words. Use each word once.
a. finale   b. eclectic   c. endure   d. transcendent   e. claustrophobia

Elaina was supposedly a marvelous decorator. My friend called her designs inspiring and (26.)_____. I was excited to see her (27.)_____ plan for my living room. First she showed me the pink walls she envisioned. They brought out a feeling of (28.)_____ in me. I felt like everything was closing in on me. Then she revealed a bright green sofa and orange chairs. I didn't think I could (29.)_____ anymore of her ideas. Still, she had her grand (30.)_____: a yellow and purple polka dot fireplace. I certainly do not have the same design tastes as Elaina or my friend.

____ 26.   ____ 27.   ____ 28.   ____ 29.   ____ 30.

Use the words below to help you match the word part to its meaning.

____ 31. -claim-: acclaim, proclaim, exclaim   a. all, everywhere
____ 32. -sens-, -sent-: consensus, dissent, sentimental   b. to feel, to be aware
____ 33. -ven-, -vent-: convene, circumvent, intervene   c. process or state
____ 34. -sis: catharsis, synopsis, hypothesis   d. to shout, to call out
____ 35. pan-: panoramic, pandemonium, pantheon   e. to come, to move toward

71

Name _____   Class _____   Date _____

Combined Quiz—Chapters 1-2

Pick the vocabulary word that best completes the sentence. Use each word once.

___ 1. The man needed a _____ person to run his business while he was gone; he had a lot of responsibilities to give the person.

___ 2. The _____ of the afternoon was disturbed when the band next door decided to practice.

___ 3. According to the _____, there is a test on Monday. I guess I should study this weekend.

___ 4. The _____ between Milt and June was apparent at their first meeting.

___ 5. Bobby's _____ behavior did not make him popular with most people. He always wanted the most of everything.

___ 6. Dan is _____ about home improvement projects. He wakes up every morning ready to work on something.

___ 7. The talent show will _____ singing, dancing, magic, and juggling acts.

___ 8. The principal told the graduating class that it _____ the best of today's youth.

___ 9. My friendship with Carlos has proven to be _____; we have known each other for 20 years.

___ 10. I try not to _____ my health by eating a lot of sweets, but I still have an occasional candy bar.

    a. serenity   ab. mercenary
    b. durable   ac. dependable
    c. zealous   ad. undermine
    d. syllabus   ae. comprise
    e. affinity   bc. exemplified

Name _____   Class _____   Date _____

Combined Quizzes—Chapters 2-3

Pick the vocabulary word that best completes the sentence. Use each word once.

___ 1. After the murder, reporters became _____ in our neighborhood. They could be found on every street waiting to ask for our opinions on the family.

___ 2. The young lovers held _____ meetings for three months before their parents discovered they were dating.

___ 3. It was a(n) _____ drive to the station after I woke up an hour late; I barely made my train.

___ 4. The meeting was extremely _____. We resolved two issues we had been discussing for months.

___ 5. When his cook refused to be _____ and insisted that the guests could not be served spoiled food, the Duke fired her.

___ 6. It is fun to visit with Angela. She is such a(n) _____ person that our chats are always pleasant.

___ 7. Jay is such a(n) _____ man that I can only spend ten minutes with him before I get depressed.

___ 8. The assistant was _____ when he pulled his boss out of the meeting to inform her about her son's accident at baseball practice.

___ 9. When I was a spy, _____ in Asia had me traveling to numerous countries, including China, India, and Thailand.

___ 10. My friend is extremely _____. When my bike broke, she was able to do an emergency repair with a hair clip and a stick of gum.

a. discreet
b. intrigue
c. amiable
d. clandestine
e. dour

ab. fruitful
ac. omnipresent
ad. resourceful
ae. submissive
bc. frenzied

73

Name _____ Class _____ Date _____

Combined Quizzes—Chapters 6-7

Pick the vocabulary word that best completes the sentence. Use each word once.

___1. I didn't like visiting Aunt Rose; she could not _____ my making a bit of a mess in her house.

___2. She was so _____ about everything. If I moved a book an inch, she noticed.

___3. Even a(n) _____ look at her hallway told visitors that this was the house of a woman who liked order.

___4. I always felt that Aunt Rose wanted to _____ me. She wanted me to be just like her.

___5. Unfortunately, I was the only person to _____ when my mom asked if we wanted to spend the weekend with Aunt Rose. My sisters got along fine with her.

___6. I was excited about going to a spa for the weekend. I was looking forward to the _____ after several busy weeks at work.

___7. The _____ in the bar was amazing when the hometown team won the championships.

___8. My sister said I needed a(n) _____ man to help me move my washer and dryer, so she was surprised when she came over and saw that I had moved them myself.

___9. The airline refused to let the woman on board because her outfit was too _____, but most of the other passengers I talked to said they didn't find her attire troubling.

___10. My mother has to _____ every story she tells so that she becomes the star in it.

    a. cursory   ab. embellish
    b. dissent   ac. euphoria
    c. precise   ad. condone
    d. seclusion   ae. provocative
    e. virile   bc. subjugate

Name _____   Class _____   Date _____

Combined Quizzes—Chapter 7-8

Pick the vocabulary word that best completes the sentence. Use each word once.

___ 1. I couldn't believe my friend was still _____ about my feelings for him. I had been dropping hints for two weeks.

___ 2. My friend said by taking me to our local museum she could show me why art is important, but I was _____. I couldn't believe that art really mattered in my life.

___ 3. People can easily _____ themselves about meeting that special someone. After a few weeks, it usually turns out that the two are completely wrong for each other.

___ 4. I _____ long weddings. I hate sitting for two hours listening to people's feelings for each other.

___ 5. _____ broke out in my house when Alfonso told my parents that he loved me; they were not fond of Alfonso.

___ 6. Before I got the test back I had a(n) _____ that I had not done well, but, luckily, my feeling turned out to be wrong.

___ 7. My fascination with scuba diving proved to be _____, but I did see a lot of beautiful sea life during the year I spent on that hobby.

___ 8. The man's _____ turned out to be true; several people had seen him sitting in the library at six o'clock.

___ 9. My friend is very _____. He is in love with someone new every week.

___ 10. I gave my _____ to the proposal only after I was sure that my kids would be safe at the neighbor's house for the weekend.

        a. delude   ab. pandemonium
        b. abhor   ac. presentiment
        c. incredulous   ad. amorous
        d. transitory   ae. oblivious
        e. alibi   bc. assent

Name _____   Class _____   Date _____

Combined Quizzes—Chapter 11-12

Pick the vocabulary word that best completes the sentence. Use each word once.

___ 1. My efforts to finish my paper were _____ at every step, from a closed
     library to a broken printer.

___ 2. People are more _____ to illnesses in the winter because they are indoors more
     often and in closer contact with others who may be sick.

___ 3. When the magazine decided to _____ responses from our readers on how they
     liked our new features, we did not expect to get five-thousand reactions.

___ 4. I _____ to a diverse exercise program: I walk, jog, or bike five times a week.

___ 5. When an animal begins to lose its _____, it will often start to explore areas occupied
     by humans.

___ 6. My friend asked me to _____ at the silent auction; I told her I would be able
     to help on Saturday evening.

___ 7. Kangaroos are _____ to Australia.

___ 8. Their friends tried to _____ a fight, but when the two men saw each other they
     could not keep the men from arguing.

___ 9. My friends and I are obviously _____. We eat everything from hamburgers to tofu.

___ 10. I am a major _____ of eating more fruits and vegetables. I always have a bowl of
     fruit on my kitchen table for guests to help themselves.

    a. advocate   ab. avert
    b. adhere   ac. habitat
    c. omnivorous   ad. impeded
    d. facilitate   ae. susceptible
    e. endemic   bc. elicit

76

Name _____   Class _____   Date _____

Combined Quizzes—Chapter 13-14

Pick the vocabulary word that best completes the sentence. Use each word once.

____ 1. My _____ of the novel was three pages long, and my friend's was a half page. I think the best summary would have been somewhere in between.

____ 2. I was surprised that my friend reads all the _____ he gets. I delete it right away; it is nothing but junk to me.

____ 3. My seven-year-old makes getting a haircut such a(n) _____ that I let it almost cover his eyes before I take him to the barber.

____ 4. I didn't appreciate the _____ as much as my colleague did. He slept in and took a later flight, but he got to the convention before me because my flight was delayed for five hours due to mechanical problems.

____ 5. I have not been _____ with security on my computer since I got a virus and had to have my computer fixed.

____ 6. Her _____ was not an appropriate way to begin a letter asking for a job. "What's sup?" did not impress the hiring committee.

____ 7. The _____ that fits this party is "dead as a doornail."

____ 8. The potential buyers used _____ in making inquiries about how badly we wanted to sell our home, but we still figured out their intentions.

____ 9. The people in my office love the FYI _____; every day I get three or four messages with these letters written at the top.

____ 10. I always check the _____ of a company if I am going to purchase an expensive item from it. I want to make sure I will have someone to consult if there is a problem.

  a. irony   ab. colloquialism
  b. lax   ac. acronym
  c. cliché   ad. synopsis
  d. spam   ae. credibility
  e. ordeal   bc. circumspection

77

Name _____   Class _____   Date _____

Combined Quiz—Chapter 17-18

Pick the vocabulary word that best completes the sentence. Use each word once.

___ 1. The _____ between the theater company and the college drama department benefited both groups.

___ 2. Memories of the disastrous concert performance when he was ten continued to _____ Stanley years later.

___ 3. The short story was a(n) _____ to Edgar Allan Poe's scary stories.

___ 4. A trip to the modern art museum proved to be a(n) _____ experience for me. I discovered several pieces of art that have inspired my own artistic creations.

___ 5. Luckily, I had the _____ to wear comfortable shoes when I spent a whole day shopping.

___ 6. Pictures of her many travels _____ the walls of my aunt's house.

___ 7. I like several works in the museum that pay homage to Michelangelo's _____ in the Sistine Chapel by representing them in different forms.

___ 8. It is a(n) _____ to share the stage with Ella; she is one of the greatest singers of all time.

___ 9. The _____ of the history museum is going to be renovated to keep up with modern tastes in architecture.

___ 10. Thieves had _____ the tomb years before the archeologist found it.

    a. adorn   ab. alliance
    b. foresight   ac. frescoes
    c. façade   ad. fertile
    d. plague   ae. homage
    e. plundered   bc. privilege

Name _____   Class _____   Date _____

Combined Quiz—Chapter 19-20

Pick the vocabulary word that best completes the sentence. Use each word once.

____ 1. The king made sure to guard his _____ well because he knew the neighboring king, his brother, wanted his land.

____ 2. I consider a low-maintenance yard a(n) _____ for a house. I hate lawn-mowing and tree-trimming.

____ 3. I like to _____ off the main routes when I travel and see areas of a town that other people don't usually see.

____ 4. After a major restoration project, the city's _____ is running well.

____ 5. I am sure I will find my _____ in the design industry soon. I have some ideas for clothing that no one else has.

____ 6. Because of King Henry's _____, his army was willing to follow him into any battle.

____ 7. I want to get rid of some of my _____, such as credit-card debt, before I buy a house.

____ 8. My deadline is _____, and I am far from done with the project.

____ 9. I admire _____. It takes a lot of courage to manage your own business.

____ 10. Maurice Hugo was merely a(n) _____ in the corporation; his family had not been in control of the company for 20 years.

      a. figurehead   ab. niche
      b. entrepreneurs   ac. liabilities
      c. impending   ad. charisma
      d. realm   ae. venture
      e. asset   bc. infrastructure

Name _____ Class _____ Date _____

Combined Quiz—Chapter 22-23

Pick the vocabulary word that best completes the sentence. Use each word once.

___ 1. I enjoyed the _____ view from the mountaintop; it was well-worth the long climb.

___ 2. The house was a(n) _____ blend of historic styles, from a medieval castle to a modern office building.

___ 3. I had to _____ many months of waiting before I found out whether I was accepted by the college.

___ 4. I couldn't give blood because I was suffering from _____.

___ 5. As a kid, I was told that reading is a(n) _____ to adventure, and throughout my life I have found that to be true.

___ 6. Construction work used to be a(n) _____ exclusively for men, but now women are often found working at construction sites.

___ 7. I was able to _____ the problem with the company after I talked to a supervisor.

___ 8. I am concerned about my _____, so I want to change some of my habits, such as eating too many fatty foods.

___ 9. We were supposed to _____ in the conference room at nine, but our manager was missing. We will try to reschedule the meeting for the afternoon.

___ 10. The doctor said a(n) _____ of vegetables in my diet was causing my health problems.

a. gateway	ab. domain
b. eclectic	ac. panoramic
c. longevity	ad. deficiency
d. endure	ae. rectify
e. convene	bc. anemia

80

Name _____ Class _____ Date _____

Combined Quiz—Chapter 24-25

Pick the vocabulary word that best completes the sentence. Use each word once.

___ 1. Telling my sister about my horrible day was a great _____ for me. I felt so much better when I hung up the phone.

___ 2. After spending two weeks camping in the wilderness, I am finding that being back in my studio apartment is leading to _____.

___ 3. It was rewarding to read the favorable reviews for my novel; I appreciated the _____ after working ten years on the project.

___ 4. My _____ was hurt when I found out that my friend had returned the gift that I had spent days picking out for her.

___ 5. The dictator made several attempts to _____ the local newspapers, but reports of his abuses kept surfacing through underground newsletters.

___ 6. I use a(n) _____ when I go into certain chat rooms on the Internet; it is fun to pretend to be someone else.

___ 7. I am beginning to suspect my neighbor of _____. When I come home, he is always peeking through his curtains.

___ 8. I still follow the _____ I was taught in elementary school: "Do unto others as you would have them do unto you."

___ 9. Yoshiko is never _____. If she doesn't like something, she comes out and says so.

___ 10. I think my friend was trying to send the _____ message that I need to clean my apartment. When we were talking about our drama class, she kept throwing in the words "dust" and "grime," which I only consciously realized later in the day.

a. subtle   ab. claustrophobia
b. suppress   ac. subliminal
c. ego   ad. catharsis
d. acclaim   ae. credo
e. pseudonym   bc. voyeurism

81

Name _____   Class _____   Date _____

Final Exam 1

Pick the vocabulary word that best completes the sentence.

___ 1. The weather forecast indicates that the _____ storm could knock out power in
several nearby communities.
a. medieval   b. dependable   c. impending   d. definitive

___ 2. My _____ was hurt when I got a C on my paper, but after I read the
instructor's comments, I understood why I deserved the grade.
a. ego   b. credo   c. euphemism   d. alibi

___ 3. My neighbor's _____ is annoying; he is always looking over the fence
when I am in the backyard.
a. domain   b. voyeurism   c. misgiving   d. humanism

___ 4. Jackie's _____ was understandable: one doesn't win a million dollars every
day.
a. voyeurism   b. serenity   c. hysteria   d. apathy

___ 5. If we make a few phone calls, I think we can _____ interest in a youth soccer
league in our area.
a. modify   b. condone   c. berate   d. elicit

___ 6. It can be hard to keep up with computer _____ because there are developments
in the field almost daily.
a. gateway   b. terminology   c. hysteria   d. zoology

___ 7. Lena is weak so often that I suggested she might be suffering from _____.
a. anemia   b. serenity   c. amnesia   d. humanism

___ 8. I don't want to be a(n) _____; as president, I am going to make some
positive changes in this club.
a. optimist   b. barbarian   c. figurehead   d. conservationist

___ 9. My friend wrote me that she wanted to visit "grease." If she continues with that
_____ error, she won't be visiting Athens, Greece, soon.
a. plague   b. realm   c. alibi   d. homonym

___ 10. There is some kind of _____ attacking students at the college; most of my classes
this week have been half full.
a. phishing   b. syndrome   c. miscalculation   d. fresco

Pick the vocabulary word that best completes the sentence. Use each word once.

____ 11. It was fun to have company, but I am tired of the _____ pace we kept up showing them the town. I am ready to relax.

____ 12. I enjoyed my time in the countryside, but I am happy to return to _____ living. I missed the shopping and theater opportunities that the city offers.

____ 13. All the nobles agreed that it was time to _____ the king. He was spending too much money on his palaces and ignoring the threats of opposing rulers.

____ 14. I want to _____ the look of the house, so I am going to repaint the trim and add new plants to the front yard.

____ 15. The _____ made the hike more interesting. I learned so much about the plants and animals in the forest and how to help save them.

____ 16. Her _____ seems to have been brought on by the shock of discovering that her mother is still alive. She can't remember anything about the last twenty years.

____ 17. The family wanted to buy a(n) _____ carpet. With six kids running over it, the carpet would have to be strong.

____ 18. We went to the revolving restaurant on the hilltop to get a _____ view of the city.

____ 19. The Spanish conquistadors _____ the Incas in Peru.

____ 20. Harold's goal was to _____ every weed in his yard. His grass was going to be perfect.

a. durable	ab. conservationist
b. annihilate	ac. subjugated
c. panoramic	ad. depose
d. frenzied	ae. amnesia
e. revitalize	bc. urban

For each set, pick the vocabulary word that best completes the sentence.

Set 1

      a. protocol   b. pseudonym   c. coup   d. ovation   e. glitch

____ 21. His friends were shocked to discover that the _____ R. Friend belonged to Tony; no one knew he had been working on a novel.

____ 22. The _____ surprised everyone. No one expected a takeover on New Year's Day.

____ 23. The wedding was very formal. The bride, groom, and family members lined up to greet us as we entered the reception according to some ancient _____.

____ 24. The biggest _____ in my plan to study all day came when my roommate returned early from her weekend trip and wanted to tell me about it.

____ 25. The street cleaners in my town deserve a(n) _____. They keep the streets so clean I really could eat off of them.

Set 2

      a. cliché   b. acclaim   c. liabilities   d. infrastructure   e. acronym

____ 26. The country's _____ was threatened by terrorist activities.

____ 27. I kept hearing the _____ ASG, but I didn't learn what it meant until someone asked me if I wanted to go to the debate sponsored by the Associated Student Government.

____ 28. The musical received _____ from old and young; it appealed to all ages.

____ 29. The _____ "as happy as a clam" fit me as I rode my bike along the country road.

____ 30. Taking all our _____ into account, I don't think we can afford a trip to Europe this summer.

Set 3

      a. avert   b. rectify   c. bewildered   d. suppress   e. dissented

____ 31. I was _____ as to why my husband said he needed to get sugar on the way home when we have a full bag in the pantry. Then I remembered that "Sugar" is the name of the dog we are pet-sitting for his co-worker.

____ 32. I wanted to _____ any argument, so I agreed to eat Thai food although I often find it too spicy.

____ 33. To _____ the problem with my new television, I have to take it back to the store.

____ 34. I _____ because I feel the plan needs to be clearer before we ask people to vote on it.

____ 35. I didn't want to _____ my feelings any longer, so I called Florence and told her how I felt.

Set 4

        a. cursory   b. discreet   c. concise   d. mercenary   e. clandestine

___ 36. After a few _____ questions to a couple of key people, I was able to discover where Jeremy had gone for the weekend.

___ 37. I don't like to appear _____, but painting the house was more work than I had anticipated, and I think I deserve twice as much money as I originally asked for.

___ 38. A _____ look through the book indicates that it is one I would like to buy.

___ 39. The couple thought they had found a place for a _____ meeting, but they saw three people they knew as they entered the restaurant.

___ 40. Her answers were just what we wanted: _____ and yet giving us all the information we needed to make a decision on whether to hire her.

Match the word to its definition.

Set 1

___ 41. edifice	a. a tendency; a leaning
___ 42. niche	b. simulated or almost existing
___ 43. impede	c. to block; to hinder
___ 44. virtual	d. a building or a structure
___ 45. propensity	e. an appropriate place or position

Set 2

___ 46. adorn	a. diverse
___ 47. plague	b. an end or halt
___ 48. moratorium	c. to decorate; to beautify
___ 49. definitive	d. a widespread disease or to annoy
___ 50. eclectic	e. most reliable or complete

Set 3

___ 51. wrest	a. to mislead; to fool
___ 52. barbarian	b. to go around
___ 53. delude	c. a savage or a person without culture
___ 54. transcendent	d. to take through force or continued effort
___ 55. circumvent	e. superior; going beyond ordinary limits

Finish the story using the vocabulary words. Use each word once.

Story 1

       a. gateway   b. adhere   c. id   d. misgivings   e. submissive

I usually (56.)_____ to strict rules of conduct, but occasionally I falter. Sometimes I am too (57.)_____ and do what others want. My cousin's behavior is usually the (58.)_____ to trouble, so I don't know why I agreed to go swimming in the lake at midnight. I had (59.)_____ about the adventure from the beginning. What I think happened was that my (60.)_____ wanted a night of freedom, and I gave into my primitive, pleasure-loving side.

    ___ 56.   ___ 57.   ___58.   ___ 59.   ___ 60.

Story 2

       a. abhor   b. innate   c. amiable   d. façade   e. catharsis

I am usually a very (61.)_____ person. I (62.)_____ conflict. I think being agreeable is a(n) (63.)_____ part of me. My mother said that even as a child, I rarely cried or became angry. When I am upset, I put on a brave (64.)_____ and pretend to be happy because people are so used to seeing me that way. I know that expressing one's emotions provides a much needed (65.)_____, so I pour out my feelings in a journal.

    ___ 61.   ___ 62.   ___ 63.   ___ 64.   ___ 65.

Story 3

       a. aversion   b. convened   c. exemplified   d. homage   e. unparalleled

When my book group (66.)_____, I was shocked to hear that several people found the book pointless or boring. The book is a wonderful (67.)_____ to the American pioneer. On almost every page, I found a story that (68.)_____ the rugged spirit of the pioneers and showed the struggles they faced in settling such a huge country. I think some people in the club just have an unreasonable (69.)_____ to nonfiction. For me, the book is a(n) (70.)_____ success and a magnificent tribute to the strong nature that has made the United States a thriving country.

    ___ 66.   ___ 67.   ___ 68.   ___ 69.   ___ 70.

Use the words below to help you match the word part to its meaning.

___ 71. anti-: antipathy, antidote, antiseptic   a. hard
___ 72. -ia: hysteria, euphoria, amnesia   b. against
___ 73. -dur-: durable, obdurate, endure   c. all
___ 74. -cred-: credibility, credo, incredulous   d. condition
___ 75. omni-: omnipresent, omnipotent, omnivorous e. to believe, to trust

Finish the sentence by inserting the correct word part. Look for the word part's meaning in each question to help you make the connection.

    a. ology   b. pend   c. cis   d. ven   e. pan

___ 76. I was handed a note that the committee would need to come together one more time before the end of the conference. The last meeting will con_____e Friday at noon.
___ 77. My im_____ing yearly review is hanging over me. I can't wait for it to be over.
___ 78. I am so glad I decided to major in zo_____; the study of animals is fascinating.
___ 79. I need to be more con_____e. People constantly say to me, "cut to the chase" or "get to the point."
___ 80. Kids were chasing each other everywhere, and the music was blaring. I couldn't stand the _____demonium at the party, but the kids were having a great time.

87

Name _____   Class _____   Date _____

Final Exam 2

Pick the vocabulary word that best completes the sentence.

____ 1. The first flowers blooming _____ that spring is near.
      a. decipher   b. modify   c. indicate   d. berate

____ 2. When the _____ reopened the movie theaters, people were a lot happier with
      their leaders.
      a. regime   b. antidote   c. niche   d. optimist

____ 3. We need several people to _____ before, during, and after the event.
      a. avert   b. embellish   c. impede   d. facilitate

____ 4. The more I learn about advertising, the better I understand how _____
      messages are used.
      a. submissive b. frenzied   c. subliminal   d. endemic

____ 5. To _____ a love of writing in the students, the school is offering a creative
      writing program after school.
      a. berate   b. nurture   c. suppress   d. assent

____ 6. I don't know why I am so _____ to colds and why my friend never gets sick.
      a. virile   b. lax   c. cursory   d. susceptible

____ 7. I was _____ about cleaning the house all winter. Now that spring is here I will be
      stricter about keeping the house fresh and sparkling.
      a. lax   b. zealous   c. urban   d. submissive

____ 8. It was sad to see how the temple had been _____ and how many of the
      statues were destroyed in the process.
      a. imposed   b. plundered   c. deciphered   d. bewildered

____ 9. The school couldn't _____ such loud and rude behavior on a fieldtrip. The offending
      students will not be allowed to go on the next trip.
      a. elicit   b. depose   c. condone   d. delude

____ 10. I enjoyed the _____ musical. I liked the experimentation of having members
      of the audience sing most of the songs.
      a. medieval   b. discreet   c. decisive   d. avant-garde

Pick the vocabulary word that best completes the sentence. Use each word once.

____ 11. I am sure I am suffering from a vitamin _____. I will check with my doctor next week.

____ 12. I was worried about my job when the company's director used the _____ "restructuring." The last place I worked fired 300 workers during "restructuring."

____ 13. I was grateful to my _____ for keeping me at work on my research paper all weekend, instead of letting me party.

____ 14. I was surprised that Kate is now _____. I thought she was still a vegetarian.

____ 15. I like to _____ the stories I tell people about my life. It is more fun to hear about me when I exaggerate a bit.

____ 16. Frank and Fran are such _____ cooks that every time we eat at their house we can expect ten different main dishes.

____ 17. My bedroom is my _____, and no one can tell me how to decorate it or when to clean it.

____ 18. The billboard for underwear proved to be too _____ for the town, and it was taken down after a week.

____ 19. The store manager put the new merchandise in a(n) _____ position to attract customers.

____ 20. With _____ there was not much mobility between classes; people usually stayed in the same circumstances into which they were born.

a. feudalism   ab. omnivorous
b. domain   ac. prominent
c. superego   ad. deficiency
d. euphemism   ae. provocative
e. zealous   bc. embellish

89

For each set, pick the vocabulary word that best completes the sentence.

Set 1

      a. entrepreneur   b. syllabus   c. assets   d. soliloquy e. privilege

___ 21. I was intimidated by the _____ for my biology class. It said that by the end
       of the semester, we would be experimenting with cloning.

___ 22. I enjoyed listening to the _____ because the actor had a beautiful voice.

___ 23. Creativity is one of Lynette's _____. Her parties are fun to attend because
       she always does something different.

___ 24. It was a(n) _____ to meet Annabel Andrews. She is my favorite author.

___ 25. My uncle is a marvelous _____. He owns five prosperous florist shops.

Set 2

      a. precise   b. subtle   c. decisive   d. pensive   e. covert

___ 26. The accident called for _____ action; my dad called 911 right away.

___ 27. I had to be very _____ with my wording to make my point clear.

___ 28. I wouldn't be a good spy. I am sure I would start giggling during a _____
       operation because I always do so when I have something to hide.

___ 29. The change in his hairstyle was _____; nevertheless, it made Juan look ten
       years younger.

___ 30. My niece was _____ before starting kindergarten. She spent the day thinking
       about what school would be like.

Set 3

      a. surpassed   b. undermining   c. proclaimed   d. endowed   e. intrigued

___ 31. The ad _____ the stars of this year's county fair: the rabbit and the green bean.

___ 32. My sister is _____ with a lovely singing voice, whereas my talents are in art.

___ 33. I _____ my goal. I wanted to do a fifty-mile bike ride, and I was able to do sixty.

___ 34. I was _____ by the title of the movie, but the film turned out to be rather dull.

___ 35. As I sat waiting for the interviewer to call my name, I kept _____ my
       confidence by thinking of ways I was unqualified for the job

Set 4

      a. zenith   b. zoology   c. realm   d. encroachment   e. irony

___ 36. In the _____ of science, Copernicus, Newton and Curie are well-known names.

___ 37. The _____ was that Tom wanted to divorce his wife after a year when he had
       pursued her for six years.

___ 38. The _____ of my college life came when I was given the "Student of the Year"
       award by the French department.

___ 39. I was confused in _____ class by all the ways animals can be categorized.

___ 40. The _____ of the housing development into the hills will force some animals
       to leave their usual habitats.

Match the word to its definition.

Set 1

___ 41. credo   a. a formula of belief
___ 42. fruitful   b. worldly
___ 43. habitat   c. dislike
___ 44. secular   d. successful
___ 45. antipathy   e. surroundings

Set 2

___ 46. holistic   a. to examine carefully
___ 47. ordeal   b. an association
___ 48. scrutinize   c. to increase in number; to grow
___ 49. proliferate   d. non-traditional healthcare
___ 50. alliance   e. a harsh test or experience

Set 3

___ 51. claustrophobia   a. stopping and beginning again; irregular
___ 52. colloquialism   b. trustworthiness; believability
___ 53. advocate   c. an expression used in informal language
___ 54. intermittent   d. a fear of small or enclosed places
___ 55. credibility   e. to recommend

Finish the story using the vocabulary words. Use each word once.

Story 1:   a. fertile   b. circumspection   c. defraud   d. venture   e. jovial

My friend is such a (56.)_____ guy that it is hard to believe anyone would want to cheat him. But when he started a new business (57.) _____, he unfortunately met some dishonest people. They were able to (58.)_____ him by pretending to have a coupon magazine where he could advertise his new restaurant. He gave them some money, and he never heard from them again. I used some (59.) _____ to discover if other business owners nearby had also been tricked, and I found out that several of them had. The (60.)_____ criminal mind keeps finding ways to deceive people, so the rest of us have to be cautious.

___ 56.   ___ 57.   ___ 58.   ___ 59.   ___ 60.

91

Story 2: a. charisma b. endure c. consensus d. synopsis e. incredulous

My children were (61.)_____ when I told them I was taking a bicycle trip across the United States. They didn't believe I could handle such a trip since I was in my sixties. I thought a bicycle would be the perfect way to see the country up close. They tried to tell me about the problems I would have to (62.)_____, such as hills, flat tires, and bad weather. I told them that with my (63.)_____, I could find help if I needed it. They laughed and agreed. We finally came to a (64.)_____ on how best to deal with problems I might encounter. I also agreed to use my laptop to send them an informative (65.)_____ of every day's ride.

___ 61.   ___ 62.   ___ 63.   ___ 64.   ___ 65.

Story 3: a. imposes b. amorous c. longevity d. optimist e. obsession

My boyfriend and I have our (66.)_____ moments, but we also have our disagreements. I am a(n) (67.)_____. I am sure that everything will turn out fine, so I like to do things without planning. My boyfriend, however, has a major (68.)_____ for time lines. He makes up a chart of what we will be doing every hour on the weekends. He (69.)_____ so many restrictions on me that sometimes I could scream. I have major doubts about the (70.)_____ of our relationship.

___ 66.   ___ 67.   ___ 68.   ___ 69.   ___70.

Use the words below to help you match the word part to its meaning.

___ 71. trans-: transcendent, transfer, transitory	a. end; limit
___ 72. -fin-: definitive, affinity, finale	b. process or state
___ 73. -sis: catharsis, synopsis, hypothesis	c. to bring, to carry
___ 74. circum-: circumspection, circumvent, circumnavigate	d. across
___ 75. -fer-: fertile, offer, proliferate	e. around, on all sides

Finish the sentence by inserting the correct word part. Look for the word part's meaning in each question to help you make the connection.

a. vers   b. am   c. ify   d. sent   e. mis

_____ 76. To make sure I made it to the meeting on time, I called the organizer to clar_____ what time it began.

_____ 77. I felt something was wrong, and my _____giving was right. We went to the party on the wrong night.

_____ 78. I love it when my husband gives me flowers and chocolate; he knows how to put me in a(n) _____orous mood.

_____ 79. My a_____ion to vegetables forced me to turn away as I passed the spinach and cooked carrots in the cafeteria line.

_____ 80. It was easy to feel the same as the rest of the board that Miami was the perfect place for our January conference. I quickly as_____ed to a week away from the snow.

92

ANSWER SECTION

Getting Started

Using Guide Words:
1. 976   2. 975   3. 157   4. 1480   5. 435
6. 655   7. 159   8. 976   9. 654   10. 654

Entry Identification:
1. entry word   2. pronunciation   3. part of speech   4. spelling of different forms
5. most common definition   6. used in a sentence   7. additional definition and sentence
8. etymology   9. synonyms

Chapter 1

Self-Test 1: 1. c   2. e   3. d   4. a   5. b   6. j   7. i   8. g   9. h   10. f

Self-Test 2:
1. durable   2. comprise   3. syllabus   4. undermine   5. zealous
6. terminology 7. indicate   8. bane   9. berate   10. apathy

Self-Test 3:
1. apathy   2. syllabus   3. berate   4. indicate   5. terminology
6. comprise   7. zealous   8. durable   9. undermine   10. bane

Context Clue Mini-Lesson 1:
1. friendly   2. scold   3. obedient   4. joy

Quiz 1: 1. c   2. b   3. d   4. b   5. b   6. a   7. d   8. a   9. d   10. c
Quiz 2: 1. b   2. e   3. a   4. d   5. c   6. d   7. c   8. a   9. e   10. b

Chapter 2

Self-Test 1:
1. happy   2. aggressive   3. dislike   4. distort   5. confusion
6. failure   7. foolish   8. generous   9. careless   10. mean

Self-Test 2:
1. affinity   2. dependable   3. exemplify   4. serenity   5. amiable
6. dour   7. submissive   8. discreet   9. fruitful   10. mercenary

Self-Test 3:
1. fruitful   2. discreet   3. submissive   4. affinity   5. amiable
6. serenity   7. dour   8. dependable   9. mercenary   10. exemplify

Quiz 1: 1. b   2. c   3. d   4. b   5. d   6. a   7. b   8. a   9. a   10. c
Quiz 2: 1. b   2. e   3. c   4. a   5. d   6. c   7. b   8. e   9. a   10. d

94

Chapter 3

Self-Test 1: 1. b 2. d 3. e 4. a 5. c 6. i 7. h 8. f 9. j 10. g

Self-Test 2: 1. ovation 2. frenzied 3. clandestine 4. glitch 5. aversion
6. omnipresent 7. protocol 8. virtual 9. intrigue 10. resourceful

Self-Test 3: 1. e 2. d 3. b 4. a 5. c 6. h 7. j 8. i 9. f 10. g

Quiz 1: 1. b 2. c 3. a 4. d 5. d 6. d 7. b 8. a 9. e 10. c
Quiz 2: 1. c 2. a 3. e 4. d 5. b 6. a 7. e 8. c 9. b 10. d

Chapter 4

Self-Test 1:
1. antiwar 2. exclaim 3. ordinary 4. concise 5. celebrity
6. magnify 7. obdurate 8. circumvent 9. infinite 10. transmit

Self-Test 2: 1. around 2. connected with 3. hard 4. against 5. cut
6. across 7. call out 8. state of being 9. make 10. end

Self-Test 3: 1. ary 2. circum 3. trans 4. dur 5. ify 6. ity 7. anti 8. claim 9. cis 10. fin

Self-Test 4: 1. h 2. e 3. a 4. d 5. j 6. c 7. f 8. b 9. g 10. i

Self-Test 5: 1. c 2. b 3. d 4. a 5. e 6. h 7. i 8. g 9. j 10. f

Quiz 1: 1. b 2. ac 3. e 4. d 5. ab 6. a 7. c 8. bc 9. ae 10. ad
Quiz 2: 1. ac 2. b 3. e 4. a 5. ab 6. d 7. c 8. ad 9. ae 10. bc

Chapter 5

Art: 1. syllabus 2. berate 3. aversion 4. ovation 5. serenity 6. dour

Self-Test 1: 1. c 2. a 3. d 4. d 5. a

Self-Test 2: 1. b 2. d 3. e 4. a 5. c

Self-Test 3:
1. aversion 2. apathy 3. exemplified 4. undermine 5. durable
6. resourceful 7. frenzied 8. submissive 9. dependable 10. affinity

Crossword Puzzle:
Across: 1. virtual 6. undermine 7. discreet 10. exemplify 13. indicate 15. clandestine
Down: 2. affinity 3. omnipresent 4. amiable 5. comprise 8. submissive 9. glitch
11. bane 12. zealous 14. intrigue

95

Quiz 1: 1. c 2. d 3. b 4. a 5. d 6. d 7. c 8. b 9. b 10. d 11. d 12. c 13. e 14. a 15. b
16. c 17. b 18. e 19. d 20. a 21. c 22. d 23. e 24. b 25. a 26. e 27. a 28. c 29. b
30. d 31. c 32. e 33. a 34. b 35. d

Quiz 2: 1. d 2. c 3. d 4. b 5. a 6. b 7. d 8. a 9. c 10. d 11. e 12. b 13. c 14. a 15. d
16. b 17. d 18. e 19. c 20. a 21. c 22. e 23. b 24. a 15. d 26. b 27. e 28. d 29. c
30. a 31. e 32. b 33. a 34. d 35. c

Chapter 6

Self-Test 1:
1. subjugate 2. cursory 3. miscalculation 4. condone 5. omnipotent
6. annihilate 7. antipathy 8. emissary 9. precise 10. dissent

Self-Test 2:
1. antipathy 2. emissary 3. miscalculation 4. condone 5. annihilate
6. precise 7. subjugate 8. cursory 9. dissent 10. omnipotent

Self-Test 3:
1. annihilate 2. antipathy 3. cursory 4. emissary 5. dissent
6. miscalculation 7. omnipotent 8. precise 9. subjugate 10. condone

Context Clue Mini-Lesson 2: possible definitions, antonym in parentheses
1. frown (smile) 2. angered (calm) 3. sad, unhappy (cheer) 4. leave (remain)

Word Part Reminder: word(s) to circle in parentheses
1. fy (to make) 2. trans (across) 3. cis (to cut) 4. dur (hard)

Quiz 1: 1. b 2. d 3. b 4. b 5. a 6. c 7. b 8. a 9. a 10. d
Quiz 2: 1. c 2. d 3. b 4. a 5. e 6. b 7. d 8. a 9. e 10. c

Chapter 7

Self-Test 1:
1. attentive 2. boring 3. weak 4. adore 5. trust
6. sadness 7. peace 8. exposure 9. cold 10. minimize

Self-Test 2:
1. amorous 2. seclusion 3. pandemonium 4. virile 5. oblivious
6. provocative 7. euphoria 8. delude 9. abhors 10. embellish

Self-Test 3:
1. euphoria 2. abhor 3. oblivious 4. delude 5. amorous
6. seclusion 7. virile 8. embellish 9. provocative 10. pandemonium

96

Quiz 1: 1. b   2. d   3. a   4. c   5. d   6. b   7. a   8. c   9. d   10. a
Quiz 2: 1. d   2. a   3. e   4. b   5. c   6. d   7. a   8. b   9. e   10. c

Chapter 8

Self-Test 1:
1. decisive 2. covert   3. transitory   4. incredulous   5. alibi
6. assent   7. circumvent   8. misgivings 9. presentiment   10. optimist

Self-Test 2:
1. assent   2. incredulous 3. alibi   4. circumvent   5. optimist
6. presentiment 7. covert   8. decisive   9. transitory   10. misgiving

Self-Test 3:
1. presentiment   2.misgivings   3. assented   4.incredulous 5. decisive
6. covert   7. alibi   8. circumvent 9. transitory   10. optimist

Quiz 1: 1. d   2. d   3. a   4. c   5. b   6. c   7. d   8. b   9. e   10. a
Quiz 2: 1. c   2. b   3. d   4. e   5. a   6. d   7. c   8. b   9. a   10. e

Chapter 9

Self-Test 1:
1. misuse   2. controversy 3. credible   4. plagiarism   5. astrology
6. omnipotent 7. expensive   8. subterranean   9. zoologist   10. sensitive

Self-Test 2:
1. feels   2. wrong   3. trusts   4. below   5. practice
6. to turn   7. hanging   8. all   9. a person   10. the study of

Self-Test 3:
1. ist   2. ology   3. sup   4. omni   5. pend
6. sent   7. cred   8. mis   9. ism   10. vert

Self-Test 4: 1. d   2. g   3. a   4. e   5. j   6. c   7. h   8. b   9. i   10. f

Self-Test 5: 1. d   2. c   3. e   4. a   5. b   6. g   7. i   8. f   9. j   10. h

Word Groups: 1. subliminal 2. suppress 3. voyeurism 4. pseudonym   5. subtle
other possibilities: seclusion, delude, euphemism, and amnesia

Quiz 1: 1. c 2. a 3. d 4. ac 5. e 6. ad 7. bc 8. ae 9. ab 10. b
Quiz 2: 1. d 2. a 3. c 4. e 5. bc 6. ad 7. ac 8. b 9. ae 10. ab

Chapter 10

Art: 1. seclusion   2. virile   3. transitory   4. covert   5. dissent   6. subjugate

Self-Test 1: 1. c   2. a   3. d   4. d   5. c
Self-Test 2: 1. b   2. c   3. e   4. a 5. d

Self-Test 3:
1. misgivings   2. amorous   3. cursory   4. delude   5. oblivious
6. condone   7. covert   8. miscalculated   9. assent   10. transitory

Crossword Puzzle:
Across: 1. provocative 3. cursory 4. annihilate 7. pandemonium 6. delude 8. euphoria
              9. alibi 10. misgiving 11. precise 12. antipathy
Down: 2. incredulous 5. presentiment 6. decisive 7. dissent   9. abhor

Quiz 1: 1. c   2. d   3. b   4. d   5. a   6. d   7. d   8. c   9. b   10. b   11. c   12. e
13. d   14. a   15. b   16. b   17. a   18. d   19. e   20. c   21. b   22. e   23. a   24. d
25. c   26. e   27. c   28. a   29. b   30. d   31. c   32. c   33. a   34. d   35. b

Quiz 2: 1. b   2. d   3. c   4. b   5. a   6. b   7. b   8. a   9. b   10. d   11. d   12. a
13. c   14. b   15. e   16. d   17. c   18. b   19. e   20. a   21. b   22. e   23. a   24. c
25. d   26. b   27. d   28. e   29. a   30. c   31. d   32. b   33. a   34. c   35. e

Chapter 11

Self-Test 1:
1. facilitate   2. oppose   3. choose 4. hinder   5. impede
6. release   7. fail   8. learned   9. unlikely 10. resistant

Self-Test 2:
1. adhere   2. nurtured   3. impedes   4. facilitates   5. advocate
6. susceptible 7. innate   8. potential 9. impose   10. surpassed

Self-Test 3:
1. adhere   2. innate   3. potential 4. facilitate   5. advocate
6. nurture   7. surpassed   8. imposed   9. susceptible   10. impeded

Context Clue Mini-Lesson 3: possible definitions
1. grand, impressive 2. meal 3. constant, nonstop 4. destroy, intrude

Word Part Reminder: word(s) to circle in parentheses
1. ist (a person who) 2. sent (to feel) 3. mis (wrong) 4. pens (to pay)

Quiz 1: 1. c   2. d   3. b   4. a   5. c   6. a   7. b   8. d   9. d   10. b
Quiz 2: 1. d   2. b   3. a   4. e   5. c   6. d   7. b   8. a   9. e   10. c

98

Chapter 12

Self-Test 1:
1. moratorium 2. mammals 3. zoology   4. elicit   5. encroachment
6. habitat   7. avert   8. omnivorous   9. endemic   10. conservationist

Self-Test 2:
1. elicit   2. mammal   3. avert   4. conservationist 5. habitat
6. endemic   7. omnivorous   8. encroachment   9. zoology   10. moratorium

Self-Test 3:
1. habitat   2. moratorium 3. conservationist 4. avert   5. mammal
6. elicit   7. omnivorous   8. encroachment   9. endemic   10. zoology

Quiz 1: 1. a   2. b   3. d   4. c   5. d   6. e   7. d   8. c   9. a   10. b
Quiz 2: 1. c   2. a   3. b   4. e   5. d   6. e   7. d   8. c   9. a   10. b

Chapter 13

Self-Test 1: 1. F   2. F   3. T   4. F   5. F   6. T   7. T   8. T   9. F   10. F

Self-Test 2: 1. lax   2. defraud   3. decipher   4. validity   5. adage
6. ordeal   7. circumspection   8. credibility 9. phishing   10. spam

Self-Test 3:
1. defraud   2. circumspection 3. credibility 4. decipher   5. ordeal
6. phishing   7. spam   8. validity   9. lax   10. adage

Quiz 1: 1. c   2. b   3. a   4. d   5. b   6. a   7. b   8. c   9. d   10. c
Quiz 2: 1. c   2. a   3. b   4. e   5. d   6. d   7. c   8. a   9. e   10. b

Chapter 14

Self-Test 1: 1. clichés   2. concise   3. euphemisms 4. acronyms 5. colloquialism
6. homonym 7. scrutinize   8. synopsis 9. bewildered   10. irony

Self-Test 2: 1. scrutinize   2. irony   3. homonym   4. colloquialism 5. concise
6. cliché   7. euphemism   8. acronym   9. synopsis   10. bewilder

Self-Test 3: 1. T   2. T   3. T   4. F   5. F   6. T   7. F   8. F   9. F   10. T

Context Clue Mini-Lesson 4: possible definitions
1. small part, portion   2. baby, overprotect   3. reject   4. complicated, difficult

Quiz 1: 1. d   2. c   3. d   4. b   5. a   6. c   7. a   8. e   9. d   10. b
Quiz 2: 1. e   2. b   3. c   4. a   5. d   6. d   7. e   8. a   9. c   10. b

99

Chapter 15

Self-Test 1:
1. donor   2. hypothesis   3. eulogy   4. intervene   5. panorama
6. dismiss   7. inertia   8. conference 9. virile   10. amorous

Self-Test 2:
1. sent   2. all   3. to give   4. bring   5. good
6. process   7. love   8. pertaining to   9. condition   10. to come

Self-Test 3: 1. fer 2. am 3. ven 4. ile 5. sis 6. don 7. eu 8. ia 9. pan 10. mit

Self-Test 4: 1. j   2. d   3. g   4. b   5. f   6. i   7. e   8. h   9. a   10. c

Self-Test 5: 1. d   2. c   3. a   4. b   5. e   6. i   7. h   8. j   9. f   10. g

Quiz 1: 1. b   2. ac   3. a   4. d   5. ae   6. ad   7. bc   8. ab   9. e   10. c
Quiz 2: 1. ac 2. b   3. c   4. ae 5. d   6. ad   7. bc   8. e   9. ab 10. a

Chapter 16

Art: 1. encroachment 2. spam 3. omnivorous 4. impede 5. homonyms 6. advocate

Self-Test 1: 1. c   2. b   3. c   4. c   5. a

Self-Test 2: 1. b   2. c   3. e   4. a   5. d

Self-Test 3: 1. potential 2. nurture   3. habitat 4. lax 5. decipher   6. acronyms
7. colloquialisms 8. avert 9. ordeal 10. innate   11. zoology   12. concise

Crossword Puzzle:
Across: 2. susceptible 4. ordeal 6. advocate   7. omnivorous 9. habitat 14. impede
   15. circumspection 18. facilitate 19. decipher 20. elicit
Down: 1. bewilder 3. colloquialism 5. adage 8. spam 10. irony 11. encroachment
   12. acronym 13. homonyms 16. endemic 17. innate

Quiz 1: 1. b   2. d   3. c   4. d   5. a 6. d 7. a 8. c   9. a 10. c 11. e 12. d 13. c 14. a
15. b   16. d 17. e 18. c   19. a 20. b 21. c 22. e 23. b 24. a 25. d 26. e 27. c 28. a
29. d 30. b 31. b 32. d 33. e 34. c 35. a

Quiz 2: 1. b 2. c 3. b 4. d 5. c 6. d 7. d 8. b 9. a   10. b 11. b 12. d 13. a 14. e
15. c 16. e 17. c   18. b 19. a 20. d 21. d 22. e 23. b 24. a 25. c 26. b 27. a
28. e 29. d 30. c 31. b 32. d 33. e 34. c 35. a

100

Chapter 17

Self-Test 1:
1. medieval   2. homage   3. privilege   4. plundered   5. secular
6. feudalism   7. alliance   8. barbarian   9. proclaimed   10. plagued

Self-Test 2:
1. barbarian   2. plundering   3. proclaim   4. privilege   5. homage
6. secular   7. medieval   8. feudalism   9. alliances   10. plague

Self-Test 3: 1. d   2. a   3. e   4. c   5. b   6. h   7. i   8. j   9. f   10. g

Word Part Reminder: word(s) to circle in parentheses
1. mit (to send)   2. don (to give)   3. am (love)   4. ia (condition)

Quiz 1: 1. d   2. b   3. a   4. c   5. b   6. c   7. d   8. e   9. a   10. b
Quiz 2: 1. a   2. c   3. b   4. e   5. d   6. d   7. a   8. b   9. c   10. e

Chapter 18

Self-Test 1 : 1. d   2. c   3. b   4. e   5. a   6. g   7. i   8. f   9. j   10. h

Self-Test 2: 1. façade   2. intermittent   3. endow   4. fertile   5. foresight
6. cupola   7. adorn   8. fresco   9. Renaissance   10. humanism

Self-Test 3: 1. Renaissance   2. humanism   3. fertile   4. frescoes   5. endowed
6. intermittent   7. façades   8. adorned   9. cupola   10. foresight

Context Clue Mini-Lesson 5: type of context clue; possible definitions
1. examples; dishonest   2. general meaning; will, choice
3. antonym (harmony); hostility, ill will   4. synonym; damage

Quiz 1: 1. c   2. d   3. a   4. b   5. b   6. b   7. d   8. a   9. b   10. a
Quiz 2: 1. e   2. a   3. c   4. b   5. d   6. e   7. d   8. a   9. b   10. c

Chapter 19

Self-Test 1: 1. F   2. F   3. F   4. T   5. T   6. T   7. F   8. F   9. T   10. T

Self-Test 2: 1. e   2. a   3. d   4. c   5. b   6. j   7. h   8. i   9. f   10. g

Self-Test 3: 1. depose   2. realm   3. impending   4. regime   5. infrastructure
6. charisma   7. wrest   8. figurehead   9. coup d'état   10. zenith

Quiz 1: 1. c   2. b   3. d   4. a   5. c   6. d   7. b   8. e   9. a   10. c
Quiz 2: 1. c   2. b   3. e   4. d   5. a   6. c   7. d   8. b   9. a   10. e

Chapter 20

Self-Test 1:
1. a desirable thing   2. cheerful   3. a recess   4. to increase   5. a preference   6. to brave
7. one who assumes the risks of a business   8. notable   9. a disadvantage 10. vary

Self-Test 2:
1. propensity   2. venture   3. niche   4. modify   5. entrepreneur
6. jovial   7. asset   8. prominent   9. proliferate 10. liability

Self-Test 3:
1. niche   2. entrepreneur   3. modify   4. venture   5. liability
6. asset   7. prominent   8. jovial   9. propensity   10. proliferate

Quiz 1: 1. d   2. b   3. a   4. d   5. b   6. a   7. b   8. c   9. c   10. d
Quiz 2: 1. e   2. c   3. d   4. b   5. a   6. a   7. e   8. c   9. b   10. d

Chapter 21

Art: 1. niche   2. jovial   3. façade   4. cupola   5. plundering   6. infrastructure

Self-Test 1: 1. b   2. b   3. d   4. c   5. c

Self-Test 2: 1. d   2. b   3. c   4. a   5. e

Self-Test 3:
1. venture   2. proclaim   3. endowed   4. plague   5. assets   6. realm
7. adorn   8.impending 9. alliance   10. liability   11. zenith   12. fresco

Crossword Puzzle:
Across: 3. niche 4. plague 8. foresight 11. cupola 12. alliance 14. intermittent
        16. plunder 17. zenith 18. endow   19. barbarian
Down: 1. medieval 2. impending 4. propensity 5. jovial 6. infrastructure   7. coup
        9. façade 10. regime 13. venture 15. modify

Quiz 1: 1. b   2. a   3. c   4. d   5. c   6. c   7. a   8. c   9. b   10. a   11. b   12. d
13. a   14. c   15. e   16. b   17. e   18. c   19. d   20. a   21. c   22. e   23. b   24. a
25. d   26. d   27. e   28. b   29. a   30. c   31. b   32. e   33. a   34. c   35. d

Quiz 2: 1. d   2. a   3. a   4. d   5. c   6. d   7. a   8. b   9. c   10. b   11. d   12. e
13. b   14. a   15. c   16. d   17. c   18. b   19. a   20. e   21. d   22. e   23. b   24. a
25. c   26. e   27. c   28. a   29. d   30. b   31. d   32. b   33. a   34. c   35. e

Chapter 22

Self-Test 1: 1. d 2. a 3. c 4. b 5. e 6. i 7. j 8. h 9. f 10. g

Self-Test 2:
1. anemia   2. holistic   3. domain   4. deficiency   5. syndrome
6. naturopathic   7. eclectic   8. longevity   9. antidote   10. unparalleled

Self-Test 3:
1. eclectic 2. longevity 3. naturopathic 4. syndrome 5. deficiency
6. holistic 7. antidote 8. domain   9. anemia   10. unparalleled

Word Part Reminder: word(s) to circle in parentheses
1. vert (to turn) 2. cred (believe) 3. fin (limit) 4. vent (to come)

Quiz 1: 1. c 2. a 3. b 4. d 5. b 6. d 7. c 8. b 9. a 10. c
Quiz 2: 1. e 2. b 3. a 4. c 5. d 6. c 7. d 8. b 9. e 10. a

Chapter 23

Self-Test 1:
1. urban   2. endure   3. panoramic 4. rectify   5. edifice
6. convene 7. definitive 8. consensus 9. revitalize 10. gateway

Self-Test 2:
1. rectify   2. urban   3. consensus 4. revitalized 5. gateway
6. panoramic 7. definitive 8. edifice   9. endure   10. convene

Self-Test 3: 1. e 2. c 3. a 4. d 5. b 6. i 7. g 8. j 9. h 10. f

Quiz 1: 1. a 2. d 3. b 4. d 5. a 6. e 7. a 8. d 9. b 10. c
Quiz 2: 1. c 2. e 3. b 4. a 5. d 6. b 7. a 8. e 9. d 10. c

Chapter 24

Self-Test 1: 1. c 2. i 3. e 4. f 5. h 6. a 7. d 8. g 9. j 10. b

Self-Test 2: 1. obsession   2. voyeurism   3. ego   4. claustrophobia 5. amnesia
6. subliminal 7. suppresses 8. hysteria   9. superego 10. id

Self-Test 3:
1. amnesia   2. id   3. superego   4. subliminal   5. voyeurism
6. obsession   7. suppress 8. claustrophobia 9. hysteria   10. ego

Quiz 1: 1. c 2. b 3. a 4. c 5. d 6. b 7. c 8. e 9. a 10. d
Quiz 2: 1. c 2. b 3. e 4. a 5. d 6. c 7. a 8. e 9. d 10. b

Chapter 25

Self-Test 1:
1. pseudonym   2. finale   3. catharsis   4. subtle   5. acclaim
6. soliloquy   7. credo   8. pensive   9. transcendent   10. avant-garde

Self-Test 2:
1. avant-garde 2. credo   3. pensive 4. soliloquy   5. transcendent
6. acclaim   7. catharsis 8. finale 9. pseudonym 10. subtle

Self-Test 3:
1. transcendent   2. soliloquy   3. pensive   4. credo   5. catharsis
6. acclaim   7. avant-garde   8. subtle 9. pseudonym 10. finale

Quiz 1: 1. a 2. c 3. c 4. d 5. b 6. a 7. b 8. c 9. a 10. b
Quiz 2: 1. d 2. c 3. e 4. b 5. a 6. c 7. e 8. a 9. b 10. d

Chapter 26

Art: 1. finale 2. anemia 3. consensus 4. voyeurism 5. soliloquy 6. claustrophobia

Self-Test 1: 1. d 2. d 3. c 4. a 5. a

Self-Test 2: 1. d 2. e 3. c 4. a 5. b

Self-Test 3:
1. endure   2. acclaim   3. longevity   4. rectify 5. amnesia   6. suppressing
7. convening   8. domain   9. unparalleled 10. subtle 11. superego 12. catharsis

Crossword Puzzle:
Across: 1. consensus 3. eclectic 5. catharsis 6. finale 7. voyeurism 9. rectify
        10. ego 12. holistic 18. transcendent 19. edifice 20. naturopathic
Down: 2. soliloquy 4. claustrophobia 8. definitive 11. superego 13. convene
      14. anemia 15. credo 16. subliminal 17. longevity

Quiz 1: 1. b 2. c 3. d 4. c 5. a 6. d 7. b 8. d 9. a 10. d 11. d 12. a
13. e 14. c 15. b 16. c 17. b 18. e 19. a 20. d 21. c 22. a 23. e 24. b
25. d 26. a 27. e 28. d 29. c 30. b 31. b 32. d 33. e 34. c 35. a

Quiz 2: 1. b 2. b 3. a 4. a 5. d 6. a 7. c 8. c 9. d 10. d 11. c 12. e
13. a 14. b 15. d 16. e 17. b 18. d 19. a 20. c 21. e 22. d 23. b 24. a
25. c 26. d 27. b 28. e 29. c 30. a 31. d 32. b 33. e 34. c 35. a

Combined Quizzes

Chapters 1-2: 1. ac 2. a 3. d 4. e 5. ab 6. c 7. ae 8. bc 9. b 10. ad
Chapters 2-3: 1. ac 2. d 3. bc 4. ab 5. ae 6. c 7. e 8. a 9. b 10. ad

Chapters 6-7: 1. ad 2. c 3. a 4. bc 5. b 6. d 7. a 8. e 9. ae 10. ab
Chapters 7-8: 1. ae 2. c 3. a 4. b 5. ab 6. ac 7. d 8. e 9. ad 10. bc

Chapters 11-12: 1. ad 2. ae 3. bc 4. b 5. ac 6. d 7. e 8. ab 9. c 10. a
Chapters 13-14: 1. ad 2. d 3. e 4. a 5. b 6. ab 7. c 8. bc 9. ac 10. ae

Chapters 17-18: 1. ab 2. d 3. ae 4. ad 5. b 6. a 7. ac 8. bc 9. c 10. e
Chapters 19-20: 1. d 2. e 3. ae 4. bc 5. ab 6. ad 7. ac 8. c 9. b 10. a

Chapters 22-23: 1. ac 2. b 3. d 4. bc 5. a 6. ab 7. ae 8. c 9. e 10. ad
Chapters 24-25: 1. ad 2. ab 3. d 4. c 5. b 6. e 7. bc 8. ae 9. a 10. ac

Final Exam 1

1. c 2. a 3. b 4. c 5. d 6. b 7. a 8. c 9. d 10. b
11. d 12. bc 13. ad 14. e 15. ab 16. ae 17. a 18. c 19. ac 20. b
21. b 22. c 23. a 24. e 25. d 26. d 27. e 28. b 29. a 30. c
31. c 32. a 33. b 34. e 35. d 36. b 37. d 38. a 39. e 40. c
41. d 42. e 43. c 44. b 45. a 46. c 47. d 48. b 49. e 50. a
51. d 52. c 53. a 54. e 55. b 56. b 57. e 58. a 59. d 60. c
61. c 62. a 63. b 64. d 65. e 66. b 67. d 68. c 69. a 70. e
71. b 72. d 73. a 74. e 75. c 76. d 77. b 78. a 79. c 80. e

Final Exam 2

1. c 2. a 3. d 4. c 5. b 6. d 7. a 8. b 9. c 10. d
11. ad 12. d 13. c 14. ab 15. bc 16. e 17. b 18. ae 19. ac 20. a
21. b 22. d 23. c 24. e 25. a 26. c 27. a 28. e 29. b 30. d
31. c 32. d 33. a 34. e 35. b 36. c 37. e 38. a 39. b 40. d
41. a 42. d 43. e 44. b 45. c 46. d 47. e 48. a 49. c 50. b
51. d 52. c 53. e 54. a 55. b 56. e 57. d 58. c 59. b 60. a
61. e 62. b 63. a 64. c 65. d 66. b 67. d 68. e 69. a 70. c
71. d 72. a 73. b 74. e 75. c 76. c 77. e 78. b 79. a 80. d